: : : : : : : : : : : : : : : : : :

The Blue Hen's Chick

: :

A. B. Guthrie, Jr., in the aspen grove at Twin Lakes, 1967

: : : : : : : : : : : : : : : : : :

The Blue
Hen's Chick

: :

AN AUTOBIOGRAPHY

BY *A. B. Guthrie, Jr.*

Afterword to the Bison Book Edition
by David L. Petersen

University of Nebraska Press
Lincoln and London

: : : : : : : : : : : : : : : : :

First Bison Book printing: 1993
Most recent printing indicated by the last digit below:
10   9   8   7   6   5   4   3   2   1

Library of Congress Cataloging-in-Publication Data
Guthrie, A. B. (Alfred Bertram), 1901–
The blue hen's chick: an autobiography / by A.B. Guthrie, Jr.; intro-
duction to the Bison book edition by David L. Petersen.
p.   cm.
Originally published: New York: McGraw-Hill, 1965.
ISBN 0-8032-2149-5.—ISBN 0-8032-7038-0 (pbk.).
1. Guthrie, A. B. (Alfred Bertram), 1901—Biography. 2. Novelists,
American—20th century—Biography. 3. West (U.S.)—Social life and
customs. I. Title.
PS3513.U855Z5   1993
813′.52—dc20
92-37591
CIP

∞

"Dark Hills" reprinted with permission of The Macmillan Co. from
Collected Poems by Edwin Arlington Robinson. Copyright 1920 by The
Macmillan Co., Renewed 1948, Ruth Nivison.

TO CALLIE

CONTENTS

The Blue Hen's Chick

1

My earliest memory is of crawling under a bed and drinking a full bottle of Castoria. I can't recall the consequences.

That must have been in 1905 or 1906.

We had migrated, in 1901, from Indiana to Montana and more particularly to the raw little town of Choteau, where my father was to be the first principal of the Teton County Free High School. There were four of us then, my parents, my older sister and I.

As standards went in days antecedent to the gospel according to Columbia Teachers College, my father was well equipped for this position. He was a graduate of Indiana University and had taught several years in that state. He was bookish by nature, and, unlike many bookish men, he knew how to maintain discipline. He had the additional advantage of a wife whose intellectual interests matched his. Mother held a degree from Earlham College, a Quaker school at Richmond, Indiana.

I can only imagine their feelings when, with a small girl in tow and a baby in arms, they got off the narrow-gauge coach at a tiny station called Collins. They had never seen blanket Indians before, never beheld the rude makeshifts of early settlement, never had to reckon with what must have struck them as a body of rough and unreckoning men. They were country folk but not folk of this country. Endless, bare plains swept around them. The unfamiliar western wind drove dust into eyes and mouths. The vast sky arched over, unbroken in outline by maple or sycamore. West somewhere, about thirty miles west it was said, lay Choteau, which they had to get to by stagecoach.

If my father did indeed feel alien in these physical surroundings, it wasn't for long. He used to tell me about his first morning in Choteau.

He had arisen early and gone outside. The air he inhaled cheered him as no air had before. Five miles southward rose two lonely buttes, which in that atmosphere he estimated to be about a mile away. All up and down the western skyline stood the great blue lift of the Rocky Mountains. Benches climbed from the valley of the Teton River and to the east leveled into flatlands that ran out of sight. Overhead—you could almost say on all sides, too—was the sky—deeper, bluer, bigger than he had ever known.

He breathed the air. He looked. He heard the ring of silence. He felt somehow afloat in space. A shudder shook him, the shudder of delight. He stretched his arms wide and said aloud, "By George, I'm free!"

So he fell in love with the country at once and in a lifetime never thereafter dallied with any other. It formed the triangle in his life, this West did. He could have gone on to bigger and better positions, as Mother encouraged him to, but, save for one forlorn ten-month absence, he wouldn't budge.

My parents must have seemed odd to most of the locals. They loved books. They liked discussions and ideas. They abhorred vulgarity. They affiliated actively with that outnumbered foe of fun, the Methodist Church. Though more nearly Unitarian than Fundamentalist, they equated, or almost equated, drink and sin. And here was a small stockmen's town and a major class whose first if not quite only interests were cattle and sheep and grass. The men were hearty and outward. To many of them teaching was a sissy occupation. They frequented the saloons, often emerging noisy and profane. They transacted business there, naturally over drinks. The saloons numbered four, as against one church, two general stores and a small variety of smaller enterprises.

Though my parents made friends and earned respect, even among the uncomprehending, they were pushed in on themselves. There were exceptions, of course, but until later years introduced additions to their company, they had largely to depend on each other for excitements of the mind. That later time was pretty late, especially for my father, who was naturally reserved and had come to lean on Mother more and more.

And to lean on the country, if not for the same reasons. To lean on the great crystal reaches and stone-blue heights of the almost animate mistress. A man with two true loves had more than most—and maybe one too many.

It was fine country to grow up in. To find riches, a boy had only to go outside. Maybe he took a piece of string with him and made a noose in it and circled the noose around a gopher hole and sat back in the sun and breeze, holding the other end of the string. Presently the gopher's nose would show, then an eye, then its head; and the boy would yank the string and pull out his squealing prize.

Or the gopher wouldn't show, and the boy just sat, letting the sunshine in, feeling the touch of wind, giving rein to mind and eye; and it didn't matter much that the gopher stayed below.

There were trout in the creeks, wild ducks on the waters, prairie chickens in the buck brush, rabbits in the thickets, and all within a mile or two. Service berries ripened and, later on, chokecherries, to be eaten out of hand or picked for pies and syrups. There were swimming holes called B.V.D. or Rosy Chicken, wild flowers, birds' nests, skating places, hills for coasters, muskrats for trappers; and everywhere was room.

No need of planned play. No hanging on to Mother and asking what to do. There was always more than enough —and don't be late for supper!

There were bitter winters when the snow cried under heel, and the boy felt buoyed because he braved them. There was wood to chop and coal to carry and the horse and cow to run in or to water, and these were good, too. There were the fierce wind and the sweet one, the chinook, running free from its dark mother cloud in the west; and when, after rough weather, the cloud brooded and the wind hatched, the chilblained boy would throw his cap in the air. Here was the promise, here the assurance, and all life lay before him, the unhatched but incubating glories.

Looking back, I see one cost of this environment. In

populated places the child of field and village too often feels
unwise and outcast and wants to get back home. At least I
did. Even on a visit to Great Falls, then a town of perhaps
twenty thousand, I was uneasy. They had the biggest smokestack in the world there and buildings that dwarfed in size
and number the cluster that was Choteau. They had street-
cars and great crowds of people, each one of whom, instead
of being green like me, was surely seasoned and disdainful. I
was afraid my father might appear foolish, for on occasion he
liked to josh a little. I feared that by some word or deed I'd
betray my total ignorance. It was always with relief to me
that we started back for Choteau, and I could see the city
drawing away behind us and the smokestack shortening behind the hills.

Even today I am not quite at home with steel and stone,
but now I know that there are others like me.

We didn't go to Great Falls often, or to farther centers.
Choteau was more fun and home was more fun, even on long
winter evenings. My father would read aloud to us then, not
just to the family but also to the young friends we children
had made. They would gather after supper and lie with us
on the floor of the living room, where the Cole's Hot Blast
maintained a sometimes spasmodic warmth, and from his
seat in the Morris chair my father would reach for the book.

George Jackson and Nan Burrell would be there and
maybe Peewee Forrest and Clifton Wyatt and probably little Frankie Monroe, who was part Indian and went by the
name of Mit Waw because that was as close as he could come
to saying "Mrs. Walley," whose son was a friend of ours,
too. On occasion still others appeared, whose names are now
misty in memory.

We would munch apples, if we were lucky enough to

have any, and maybe squirm closer to the fire and never miss a word. We were in other and new worlds and even the howling of the real world's winds went unnoticed.

My father had a fine sense of theater, an elastic baritone voice and a way with dialect. When he spoke for Uncle Remus, he *was* Uncle Remus, and he was also Brer Rabbit and Brer Fox; and the scenes would unfold before us more real than coal stove and apple cores. With Mowgli and Kaa we coursed the Waingunga and died magnificently with old Akela among the dead dhole of the Dekkan. With Pitamakin we went in quest of the fish-dog skin. David Copperfield, Huck and Jim, Pip—we were all of them in that screen of the mind that no outer screen equals.

Bedtime would come, and my father would close the book.

"Please, one more chapter," we'd ask. "Please, one more story."

"Just one more, then"—and we were off again.

My mother had the reputation of being the worst housekeeper, the best cook and the most indulgent parent known. Our home was commissary, playground and frequent lodging place for the youngsters of the town. We could play bean bag and improvised basketball inside the house, whatever the weather. We could wrestle and run. We could hoot and holler. We could bounce on the beds and battle with pillows. Rarely did such roughhousing bring more than a mild and amused admonishment.

Mother never objected even when Mit Waw wanted to stay the night, though he always wet the single bed to which, with some prudence, we assigned him. In the morning she ripped off the sheets cheerfully, did the washing by hand and made ready for the next accident.

We would bang into the house for a snack or for lunch, maybe four or six or more of us; and she had squeezed in time in her busy and often burdened day to make doughnuts in quantity, or cookies, or pies, or to dip the chocolate candy that we liked best of all. She never complained and never failed us. Even without food in readiness, she managed somehow.

I am amazed and oppressed, casting back in early remembrance to her day-by-days. For water, a hand pump. For a toilet, a privy, with the complements of chambers and slop jars on frozen nights. For light, coal-oil lamps. For washing, a tub and a board. For hot water, tea kettles and buckets and the kitchen-range reservoir. For heat, the range and the coal stove. No refrigeration in those times, and no ice in summer unless in winter you had cut and stored it yourself; on hot days it was hard to tell butter from batter. We bathed in a circular washtub.

Washing. Ironing. Dusting. Pushing broom or Bissell sweeper. Cooking. Pumping. Dumping swill. Sewing. Mending. In season canning wild and brought-in fruits, for without them winter offered little but dried apples, though the merchants managed to freight in oranges as a Christmas specialty. Toting coal and firewood when we forgot or skimped our chores. By night and morning straining milk and putting it away to cool and then to skim. Churning. Making cottage cheese. Filling lamps. Trimming wicks. Polishing smoked chimneys. Putting down sauerkraut. Putting up mincemeat. Tending a baby in arms or carrying one in the womb. And all the time finding time for us who were older and for our friends.

Twenty years and more after her death I think of my mother as constant lovingkindness, and as constant, largely inward anxiety, for mortality ran so high among her children that people said privately we came of weak blood. Lovingkindness, which I took for granted, and anxiety, which I was quick to sense and share with her.

I was fourteen years old before I could spend, without distress, one night away from home. Momism, I suppose they would call it today, with no allowance for popism or brother-and-sisterism or that damned but right word here, togetherness.

Sunday was the Lord's day. It was the day of pause from play and toil, except, of course, for Mother, whose toilings didn't count. Fat Sabbath meals met heaven's favor. We went to morning worship, Sunday school and evening service, and my father slipped a hard-won silver dollar in the dish. Somewhat later, for youngsters with awakened glands, came the Epworth League, a group made solemn by the awful option of brimstone or beatitude.

Mother usually fried chicken on Sunday, a lot of it. When the garden offered, she picked squaw corn, which grew, particolored, on a small and tortured cob and was the only fresh corn that our short season could supply. She mashed potatoes, baked biscuits, made gravy. Mostly we did without green stuff, save what little could be grown or picked wild in the spring. For dessert there was pie or cobbler or cake or floating island. On banner days she had the fixings for ice cream, and, between prayers, psalms and sermons, we'd crank the old freezer, never deeming this work-and-play a violation of holy ordinance.

After Sunday school we feasted as on no other day. We'd race home, we children, with the strains of "Our Sunday School Is Over" sounding in our ears. When we grew old enough, we'd heave a chunk of ice into a gunny sack, crush it with the side of an axe, pack the freezer, and spin the crank

until, by balking, it gave the glad announcement of completion. And the dasher! Do any children these days see it lifted
from the can and scraped off? Do eager hands still grasp it,
and eager tongues lick what is left?

With ice cream off the menu, we kids would prowl the
kitchen, sniffing like coyotes, while Mother popped an apron
on to shield her Sunday dress. We'd gather at the table and
wait wolfishly while my father, who was as wolfish as the rest,
reserved the kill just long enough to render our acknowledgment.

Despite our best performances there'd often be some
chicken left. Not always. Sometimes Brother Van Orsdel,
conference superintendent of the Methodist Church, would
come to town.

Brother Van was a hearty man, part of whose reputation rested on his readiness to preach in any place, especially
saloons. He had a genuine and engaging dedication to the
church. He also had an appetite. He stays in memory, for he
liked to eat with us, as a person of two passions—faith and
food. He could weep for Jesus and rejoice for Mother's fare.
Another ear of corn, please, and a morsel more of meat! I
didn't think then, if he could chance the charge of deadly
sin, then I could, too. I just competed.

Most Sundays offered something as the hour of evening
prayer approached—leftovers of chicken we hadn't had relish or room for. My upper garb was a Buster Brown tie and
a blouse bound at the waist by a drawstring. Before we set
out afoot for devotions I'd cache in the blouse a couple of
backs or necks and maybe a wing or two and a gizzard.

In church I prayed with the rest. Offkey I sang the old
hymns, seeing afar the land that was fairer than day and the
lifeline flung to the floundering sinner. But when the minister began assaulting us, I reached for reinforcements. I ate

slyly, with my head bowed, and must have been considered uncommonly devout for one of my tender years. There, with the preacher rolling out his saving syllables, there with my chicken, I felt close to God and grateful for earth's goodies. I doubt that anyone ever was condemned for coveting chicken, even in church, provided only that he cheered.

When Mother discovered my secret, she laughed.

For all my worldly pleasure in the precincts of the spirit, indoctrination was off to a splendid start. The suds of gospel truth, applied sufficiently, brain-washed the soulful subject clean of all but God and guilt. I never quite could picture God, but He was always close about, a brooding Being who wept over His creations and loosed His awful wrath because His name was Love. Not for some years could I hazard the heresy that man, if he'd failed, was his Manufacturer's failure. It was then I commenced to think better of man. The sense of guilt abides, scar tissue of primitive Christian persuasion.

We went to the Methodist church because it was the only one to go to. It shook me later to discover that, given the choice, both my father and mother would have chosen a house less hidebound—this despite a code of conduct so starchy as to contrast with the least refinements of faith.

Until we children educated, or eroded, our parents, no word close to a swearword, even though closer to slang, was allowed to be uttered. "Lordie" was barely permitted but not "Goddie," which I tried only once. "Hell" was a name and "damnation" a noun. For exclamations, instead, my father used to use "Great Scott" and "Holy smoke," which, if near equivalents, nevertheless had been cleared. In moments of extreme exasperation he was heard to say, "The devil!" Any kind of liquor was a curse, proscribed even in cookery, though I do remember that Mother used to put a few drops of whiskey in the castor oil she dosed me with. The mixture was supposed to be less revolting than the medicine alone. It was awful, so awful that only years of hard determination made endurable even the bouquet of bourbon. Once a doctor prescribed ale for Mother, who was producing too little milk for a lately born baby. The ale was kept under the bed, where people weren't likely to peek.

We didn't play cards, not having any, though I can't recall an association there with evil. Dancing somehow enjoyed an exemption, but it came along later and may have owed something of consent to attrition. Not dancing on Sunday, though. When, in high school, we went to Saturday-night dances, we quit on the stroke of midnight, partly out of personal principle, partly out of fear of parental displeasure, but largely out of an unlabored affection for home. When movies first came to our town, we were allowed to go occasionally, but never on a Sunday.

These restrictions were lax in relation to those on the subject of sex. Spoken references here had to be so refined as almost to make vulgar, in retrospect, illustrations by way of the birds and the bees. I see my father in frowning embarrassment because in mixed company I mentioned a book called *The Fruit of the Family Tree.* I hear him telling me privately, with a hint of envy and perverse satisfaction and also a hint of a word to the unwise, that sheep, unlike humans, bred but two times a year. Sometimes I wonder if he didn't fear sex because he had too much appetite for it, too much for a man committed to monogamy. It could have been the combination of appetite and single direction that made him severe. When I was in college and old enough for such talk he told me, harking back to his bed, that a man had no right to make his woman a brood sow. By that time it was too late for all but reflection.

Delicacy drove home the awful aspect of sex. Through euphemisms we learned as youngsters that ruin lay in our pants. Destruction awaited Onan, whose name and shame I stumbled on later. To the hospital, asylum and grave went the men known to visit Eva Fox and her miserable girls who lived down by the creek in what gentility could not say was a whorehouse. And the hazard and dishonor of the taker of hymen! Living proof was apparent, in accordance with the offense, in epileptic seizures, balding heads, crippled joints and girls disgraced.

There in home and house of God I got my moral training, complete with commandments and imagined adornments here unmentioned. Yet by denominational standards my parents were heretics. When, at eighteen, I was old enough to meet but not to measure challenges of doctrine and contradictions in the Word, I found to my discomfort that neither my father nor my mother could embrace the Trinity, that they demurred mildly to the reported miracles of Jesus, that they were puzzled by a personal God, if there were one, and didn't believe in hell and maybe not even in heaven. The closest my father came to an expression of hope in the hereafter was in saying that without it life on earth was a hoax. They even gave a nod to the theory of evolution, a nod all the more startling to me because until then I hadn't imagined and couldn't imagine such unorthodoxy in either of them.

Perhaps they hadn't realized how true a believer I'd become. If they did, I assume they assumed that the excesses of Wesley would wash away with the years. Anyhow, Sunday school and church were good for youngsters. Even though the pitch of philosophy was pretty low, small harm was done and benefit abided.

I got the benefit all right. The stern injunctions, the

arguments by analogy, the proofs through infirm parallel, the glad, despairing, martial messages of hymns, the sworn truth that God lived and all was well and vengeance was His—all these I accepted and was laid low. There was home, too, with a code that gave enforcement to a creed my parents had unspoken doubts about. I used to pray and pray again, to no apparent avail.

There were other youngsters, I am sure, who were made of tougher stuff, but there were and are certainly others like me—the impressionable ones—who were and are being crippled and scarified by parents and preachers and priests who proclaim a personal God and through fear try to discipline sex. That suits fundamentalist churches just fine, I suppose. It fills the pews and puts support in the plates. It also gives needed employment to the personnel of asylums and to psychiatric workers. If I had my way, I'd be tempted, though tempted only, to rip out of the Bible all pronouncements like these: "Be ye therefore perfect" and—I conform here to the inevitable paraphrase of the primitive pulpit—, "As a man thinketh in his heart, so is he." Taken lightly, as I'd have them taken if taken at all, perhaps they're innocuous. Taken seriously, they raise the devil—and rebellion, if it comes, often carries too far.

Brothers and sisters came and went. Into the sod my parents had to lower six, all stricken young. My mother bore nine children, of whom I never saw the first. I saw the others and in childhood saw them die and saw them put away. Of nine, the most that lived at any single time were four, and those times were brief. My sister, Nina Bess, eldest then of four, at fourteen succumbed to meningitis in Southern California, where Mother had gone with us children for the health of Baby John and me. We made the cruel trip back to

Montana and into March's frozen ground put Sister, who, I told myself, was too beautiful and good and too much loved to live away from heaven. John died that autumn of the same year. The others also died in infancy, of scarlet fever, whooping cough and of what doctors of that day called, in shotgun terminology, bronchitis.

So my memory is full of funerals, of the cold, still parlor, of the cold coffin and the cold, still body lying in it. My nose is full of the stink of carnations, and my ears hear again the whine of God's-will-be-dones, and both sicken me. I'd rather smell wild onions and listen to the wind and shut from thought my wonder at the simple, fearful, maimed minds that forgive their God His trespasses.

We were always poor, I guess, or, by generous appraisal, reduced in circumstances by illness and the undertaker; but if conscious of our state at all, I was not oppressed by it. Not many possessed much money then. We had enough to eat. Our clothes were stout though few. Our sometimes leaky roof sufficed. What more could people ask, except rarely for a nickel to buy an all-day sucker? I didn't see why Mother always wanted, in some glad and distant day that never dawned, to make structural changes in the house.

Our riches, felt rather than defined, lay at home, which the fragility of our family somehow made the dearer. Despite our modest means, despite bereavements or in their temporary absences, despite my forlorn soul, despite paternal plagues that I must come to later, we had our happy and abundant times. And whether poorhouse, hell or heaven, home was home.

Added to our riches, though unreported by the bank, were the dividends the outdoors paid. Through my father's old field glasses he and I identified, with help from books, birds in our region rarely seen and more rarely recognized. We counted the Savannah sparrow, the olive-backed thrush, a brown thrasher that forsook ancestral acres in favor of the west and staked a homestead in a bullberry bush. We rejoiced at seeing these and others, at knowing more about the world around us. A weakened waxwing grew into a pet. So did a redpoll, and, when spring came on, a cottontail that at first my hand would hold. I found a mallard's nest and put the eggs beneath a hen, which followed her confusing brood along an irrigation ditch and was not seen again.

The joy of hunting was beyond accounting, once I was old enough to be trusted, if anxiously, with my father's old shotgun. I loved to bring birds down, to take quick aim at mallards, pintails, teal and prairie chickens on the wing and feel the twelve-gauge bounce against my battered shoulder and see the flight stopped short and the broken target fall.

The season opened early, soon after the school year commenced, and I spent my classroom hours impatiently, straining for three o'clock and the hours that counted. Yonder, westward, were prairie-chicken cover and beaver dams and potholes that blue- and green-winged teals frequented and, farther on, three little lakes well liked by bigger ducks.

My brother and I had done the chores at home, except for the evening milking, and that my father would attend to. There was chopped wood in the wood box, coal in the coal scuttles, no ashes in the stoves. My conscience was clear. The way was open, barred only by the crawling clock.

On dismissal I'd run home, change my clothes and grab shotgun and shells and join, or be joined by, another hunter. Oftener than not it was George Jackson, my close friend then and now, of whom I will speak later. We'd start out happily afoot, not thinking of the ten miles or more we'd cover but of the birds we'd bag.

The days were yellow, tinted by September, and though shortened from high summer still were long. Across the valley, up the slopes and on the benches the buffalo and bunch grass had turned tan, cured on the stem. Along the river the cottonwoods were fading, revealing in their leaves the veins of age. The gophers had grown fat for winter. Jackrabbits began to show the change from brown to white, to match the coming snow. A meadowlark that should have flown south sooner sounded its fall song. Flushed by frost, bullberries sparkled in their silver thickets, red as Indian beads, and chokecherries hung in fat and purple clusters among despairing leaves. The sun and sky were kind, unwilling yet to yield to winter yet touched with a surrender that made the heart glad for this final, fleeting stand. The hunting season, the first, sad, gorgeous days!

Later the wild goose would cry, the snow goose and his grander kinsman, the Canadian, and still later I would drop four of the latter from a station in a homestead privy near a lake where I fired through a broken, foot-square window while crouching on the seat; but now we were laden, now we had spoonbills or mallards or widgeons or teals or butterballs or grouse or more likely a variety, and now night was closing in. Time to go home.

We were as tired as boys could be, but we sang as we slogged along, made vocal by our accompaniment, by the good, wild smell of blood and feathers and exploded powder. We sang "Heidelberg" or "La Miserere" or "Smile the While" or "The Rose of No Man's Land" or hymns like "Beautiful Isle of Somewhere." The themes didn't matter: they were all one and all glad. We sang in the listening silence or as the chinook wind moaned around us or as the

north wind whistled, knowing we could make it home, knowing Mother would be waiting and have warmed and waiting
for us the food our stomachs cried for.

Once with a .22 I shot down two coyotes. These wily
little wild dogs are known to feed on chickens, lambs and
even calves, and so the rightful man destroys them. I had
flushed the pair from a pigweed patch at the base of a butte.
They sped angling up the slope, one to left and one to right,
and I fired left and right, once each, and flattened both. Fine
shooting, if by accident. Incredible marksmanship. I wished
with pounding pride someone had seen me.

One of the coyotes wasn't dead, I found as I walked up
to him. He lay without struggle looking at me, looking
through and beyond me, with no fear of man now in his
yellow eyes but only with the resigned and final wonder of
death. I had to put another bullet in him, this time in his
wondering brain.

No longer do I like to kill or see things killed. When
slaughter justifies itself by simple economics, I yield, although reluctantly. Sometimes, rarely, even yet, for sake of
pan and palate, I'll shoot a bird or beach a fish, but there's
little sport in either act. And I'd as soon blast any trusting
milk cow as fell an elk or deer. The watcher lives to see
watched things again, and while life maybe isn't precious, to
put an end to it is mournful.

But I would not give up my recollections, though
touched with unease in thinking of my old blood-thirst and
the crippled creatures that hid successfully and died in mis-
ery. Those days were great as of my time. I've long since
said goodbye to them, but never to remembrance.

Under outdoor assets enter fishing. My father was inexpert in matters I shall mention but equal to the best along a
trout stream. He knew where the fish would be, whether in

shallows or deeps. He could cast a Coachman or Professor just where he wanted it, without slap of line or lure. No insect on the water looked realer than his fluttering fly. We counted that day lost when we didn't get a "mess," which meant enough for supper, which meant a weighted creel.

The automobile and better roads and original sin would alter things. The bright and blue-holed Teton would have more fishermen than fish. Happily in those early days we didn't think to count the cost of progress or of blind procreation. We just hitched old Fox to the buggy and set forth, sure of our afternoon and of everlasting others.

Fox was a staggy chestnut gelding, composed one part of fire and one of fear. Whether in harness or under saddle he showed class, but so little as a wind-blown leaf would spook him, and he'd shy violently. The smell of hunting and fishing jackets terrified him, and if my father, garbed in one, got too near his rear, Fox would take a swipe at him. He was gentle with us children, though. We could climb his foreleg and straddle his bare back, two or three of us, and set out with only a twig to guide him by. My father was the only one ever to be kicked at, and this discrimination vexed him. He saw no reason for it and would retaliate in kind.

But, rolling on to fishing grounds under a gentle sun, we'd agree Fox was some horse all right, and from his pocket my father would withdraw a nickel plug of licorice and answer, grinning, to my smile; and we'd have a chaw and through blackened lips discuss the flies that fit the light, the river's stage, the season.

On great occasions we traveled up the Teton to its exit from the Rockies and on into the high-walled canyon it had scoured. It was on one of these outings that I found a crack in my father's façade.

As preparation, remember that he never swore or used a word at all close to the borderline. And throw in the fact for what it's worth that I, being dutiful and bossy with my juniors, would insist they swear to swear no more. I must have contributed much to the Lord's delight. I was sure I was so doing.

Our luck had been extraordinary. Even my younger brother, Chick, a mild, good, easy-natured boy who'd much rather swing a ball bat than a rod, had landed quite a few. By noon we had a mess and more. So we sat down on the gravel facing a fine pool and brought out sardines and crackers. For lunch on fishing trips we always took sardines. Matter of harmony, I suppose.

Something in the water caught my father's eye. There on the river bed, he said, pointing with a sardined finger, lay what might be an Indian hammer head, a squaw stone, a rock in which a circle had been nicked to accommodate the thong that would fasten head to handle. The riffles made it hard to tell.

He got up and found a long, dead limb and poked it in the water and began trying to bring the thing to shore. All at once he dropped the branch, yelled "Holy smoke!", clapped his hand to his forehead, wheeled about and began scrambling from the stream.

Chick and I jumped to our feet and dashed after him.

He halted, puffing, after twenty yards. A hot, red, growing bump showed on his brow.

"A hornet!" he said. "A fool mountain hornet!"

It was then we spied the nest, hanging gray against the farther bank.

Chick and I picked up a couple of rocks each.

"No, boys, no," my father said, looking a little sheepish

now. "Let's not bombard it." He put a gentle finger to the bump. "This wouldn't happen once in a thousand times. Just accidental. So be kind."

Reluctantly we dropped our rocks.

"I bet," my father went on presently, "I bet if we go back quietly I can get that Indian hammer out and not be stung again."

We returned with him. He retrieved the limb he'd used and resumed his nudging of the stone. A second "Holy smoke!" burst out of him. The limb fell with a splash. He slapped his head within an inch of where he'd slapped before.

We ran again, the three of us, and as we ran he shouted, word by panting word, "Rock hell out of 'em, boys! Rock the holy hell out of 'em."

In spite of my propriety I liked him better for his lapse—and felt at greater liberty.

In grade school none of us youngsters ever heard of an allowance. We weren't bothered. Anyhow, we had resources. If a boy was strong enough, he could team up with another and make some money sawing logs, which the white-and-Indian hybrids, known universally as breeds, hauled in from the mountains as fuel for Monarch ranges. The instrument was a flexible, hand-powered cross-cut which my partners in those enterprises were always bending, to my hardship, at the moment of my draw. They accused me, falsely, of the same. But when we'd sawed a load of wood we got three dollars. Or, from a shrinking housewife who had chickens in her backyard, a boy might make a dime or so by decapitating fryers. Or, for a dollar daily, he might pick potatoes. He broke his back thereby but, in course of time stood straight again. Or he could search the alleys for spent beer

bottles which, cleansed inside and out, were worth five cents
for three at the backdoors of saloons. Once in a while he
found an empty half-pint whiskey flask which alone was
worth a nickel. Such earnings in my case were kept scant by
my parents, though not so scant as they supposed.

One source of income was denied us absolutely. Periodically, according to their periods of thrift and thirst, sheep-
herders would show up in town to wet their whistles. Wet is
hardly the word; drown is closer, though still an understate-
ment. Night and day, as long as cash and credit lasted, they
kept the Old Crow flowing, and in grand, contemptuous moments showered coins around for kids to scramble for. Or
they handed silver to every boy and girl they met. We
weren't allowed to scramble or accept and felt a trifle under-
privileged. Our parents were correct, of course, but, looking
back, I have a certain sympathy for the herders' high re-
nouncements of the metallic measurements of men.

At fourteen, with grade school behind me, I took a
steady summer job as printer's devil with the weekly
Choteau Acantha, which my father formerly had owned and
unwisely sold. My beginning chores were to sweep out, to
tidy up and to sort and put away what the trade called leads
and slugs and furniture. My agreed-on compensation for a
six-day week was nothing but experience, though often at
the close of a long Saturday the owner slipped a dollar to
me. My father thought the training fine; he believed a man
should know a trade in case higher callings somehow didn't
call.

As my apprenticeship proceeded, not only in that summer but in later ones and in hours unrequired by high school,
my hands grew quick to stamp and roll the single copies of
the paper that were addressed afar. "Single wrappers," we
called them. I learned to distribute and to hand-set type, to

make up and lock up a newspaper page or piece of job work, to feed the presses, small or big. I got to be a fair hand at the linotype. A two-thirder, a journeyman printer would have labeled me.

In those years of high school, by season roughly from September into early June, I built the early-morning fires at home, milked the cow, hurried as reporter to the Great Northern station for local items on arrivals and departures, rushed to the shop and kindled heaters there, and appeared in time for class, smelling of cow and kerosene, and divided Caesar's Gaul. From school I went back to the shop and worked till six o'clock and sometimes came back after supper. I worked on Saturdays, too, and, if need be, on Sundays. I made as much as fifteen dollars a week, though seldom during hunting seasons. No matter. My money kept some friends and me in shotgun shells, with overage for billiards. Not silly pocket pool but billiards, straight-rail or three-cushion! My parents were disposed to frown on pool halls but couldn't but admit that Walter Gorham's place was hard to criticize.

I don't know how I did so much, except that I was young, or how I kept my grades up, except I was absorbent. The point is not my occupations but my earnings, which rather blinded me to needs at home. Blinded to needs, so alive with juices as to dim awareness of my doom, I was quite a squirt.

Not until years later did the hard, sore fact of parental struggle strike me down, not until after my mother had succumbed to cancer and my father, almost as if by an act of will, had thereupon grown old and year by solitary year become more senile. Successively school principal, newspaper publisher, land-and-loan company representative, county treasurer, bank cashier, then schoolman again, he never

lacked for occupations. With such little help as we could give
or, rather, did give to him, he put three of us through college; yet the most he ever made as educator was $3300 an-
nually. At the time the figure didn't seem so poor to me,
though I knew he borrowed on his insurance to keep us going
in school. Then, as his mind and memory failed, I had no
choice but to sell the small property he had managed to ac-
quire. It consisted of a frame, four-bedroom house just outside of town and thirteen acres of surrounding land on which,
with what I know now was desperation, he'd tried the sideline
venture of raising for sale as breeding stock the few head of
pure-bred sheep that his pasture would support. With the
transfer of his place about accomplished, I looked at the
abstract. In it I found he'd had to mortgage house and land
for the $300 it took to install a water system!

Well, in her later years Mother was delivered from the
hand pump and the outhouse.

2

Father was the embodiment of man-against-machine. He had small skill with it and smaller patience. He could parse a piece about mechanics and seem to understand, while snorting at its grammar, but application was beyond him and efforts at it made him bilious, convinced against his higher reason, if he ever tried to exercise it, that the devil was afoot. A horse and buggy he could handle, though when it came to lubrication of the latter the left-hand threads on left-hand axles kept confusing him. Each time he solved the secret, the why of it occurred to him, and he'd explain with a touch of the triumphant that, if threaded to the right, the nut with use would loosen and the wheel roll off its spindle. In physical direction the way to tighten or unscrew an ordinary nut was his one certainty. All his life he was perplexed at first blush about which hand was which.

The buggy fell to pieces finally, and old Fox lost his fire and fear and died. Anyhow, the machine age was upon us. Our first car was a Model T, our second one a Dodge. By the time that Father bought the former—a used number with vagaries he regarded as hostile and premeditated—I had learned something about driving a Ford, having toured a time or two in one owned by the parents of a friend. Father never had had his hands on a wheel. On that first day of ownership I demonstrated and explained.

"Simple," Father said, though he had the look of a man about to face a trial. He hated the thought and fact of being "rattled," as he put it, perhaps because implements so often rattled him. "Nothing to it. Move around, Son."

He took the wheel. He pulled the throttle lever down to the point at which the fenders pranced. Then he jammed the first-gear pedal down.

It happened that Choteau was installing its first water system. To left and right of the unpaved street ahead of us were trenches that awaited pipes.

With a great scratch of gravel the Model T took off, bound for the open tunnel to the left.

"Right!" I yelled. "Right!"

Father was glued to the wheel. His foot was glued to the pedal. His eyes bulged.

I shouted "Right!" to him again.

He cut farther left.

The hungry trench sped at us.

I hit Father on the arm and screamed above the clatter, "This hand!"

He wrenched the wheel around, his foot still glued to low, his eyes still popped.

Now, from almost dead ahead, the right-hand trench advanced.

I doubt he heard me when I cried, "Straighten up! Left now! Straighten!"

In any case he never straightened. We careened down the street, from trench edge to trench edge, and plowed into a sandpile for which I'd tardily prepared by reaching over and shoving up the hand throttle.

We got out. Looking baleful, Father sized up the baleful Model T. "Well!" he said. "Well!"

The Model T stayed with us for four years or so. Father had paid $300 for it and was not about to give it up or admit he'd had enough.

Winter tested his mettle. When the temperature fell to zero or below, the Ford decided to sleep the season through, and the most heroic efforts often failed to break its sullen slumber. It had to be hand-cranked, of course, hand-cranked with one hand, without push or pull or anchor from the other, which had to occupy itself with a choke wire that protruded from the grill. We called cranking "twisting her tail." We called choking "goosing." In innocence, too. It was years before I knew another meaning of the term.

On cold mornings when we needed transport, before I was strong enough to twist her tail myself, Father prepared for combat by looking grim and speaking short. At zero hour he'd take a boiling bucket, go out, and pour the water in the radiator. Though he knew the war had just begun, he'd take a few heaves at the crank, just in case of miracles. No miracle. He'd jack up a hind wheel. This made the cranking somewhat easier, if easy is a word for next-to-utmost effort, and protected him besides. By some sly alliance of engine and wheels the machine, though out of gear, would charge you when awakened. Outside, it tried to run you down. In the buggy shed that did for a garage it squashed you against the wall. It did, that is, unless you'd hoisted up one of its hind legs.

When these tactics didn't win, Father twisted out the spark plugs and poured raw gas in the cylinders. He had a final weapon if these tactics failed. He'd come inside and fire the blowtorch—no simple task for him—and go back to heat the intake manifold. Sufficiently exasperated, he'd put the torch not only to the manifold but to almost all the goddam engine. (My adjective).

Except when I went out to help him if I could, we all waited in the house, knowing sun or storm would enter. Often it was storm. The son of man had gone down before the forces of evil and was not pleased with anyone about it.

The Dodge had a starter, four-gear shift and foot accelerator, and Father found it complicated beyond the complications of the Ford. The shift didn't bother him by being irregular, with low where reverse was in most makes and other gears accordingly displaced. It plain bothered him. He had labored mightily to master the Model T's simplicities and, having learned a thing or two, resented or was always ready to resent what people called improvements. Why a foot throttle when a hand throttle did as well or better? Where was the infernal button that gave impulse to the starter? With the Dodge you had to turn a key to excite its nervous system. Sometimes he forgot to turn it, and sometimes, ready to start off, he found he'd left it in the house. In either case he wasn't happy. With the Ford there'd been a fixed switch underneath the coil box, and all a man need do was slide it to magneto. When he got the Dodge to perking, he'd rev the engine, throw the thing in one gear or another, and thunder off. Often he forgot to shift from low and went to town in roaring smoke.

One morning he went out to start the Dodge and get himself to school. From the house I watched him through a window. I saw, or saw enough to know, that his foot came up, then pressed, came up and pressed again, and saw annoyance mounting in him.

I went outside to see if I could help. Before I reached him, he flung himself from the contraption and slammed the door.

"Deader'n a mackerel!" he said in deadly tones. Then he turned and gave the thing a rightful kick, putting a dent in the body.

He hadn't pressed the infernal button. He'd been pushing on the throttle.

In the days of my childhood nearly every householder kept a little bunch of chickens. Mostly the birds were nondescript, though here and there you'd find a flock of Rhode Island Reds or Plymouth Rocks or Brown Leghorns.

I don't know how or why Father made his choice, but what he got eventually were pure-bred Silver-Laced Wyandottes—a name by itself more impressive than any except perhaps for Buff Orpingtons. We would have argued that point if there had been any of the latter around.

It was the name, I think, that made us proud, for there was no proof of superiority in our hens unless you counted appearance. The laces of silver against the backgrounds of black made them handsome.

But we had one superior rooster!

I did not know his qualities until, returning from one of the early grades of grammar school one afternoon, I found him fighting a rugged Rhode Island Red that had apparently tired of his lot and gone looking for lacy additions.

Obviously the fight had been long. Both roosters were winded and bloody. My boy had the challenger down and was trying, though weakly, to peck out an eye. As he waited an instant for wind and the strength to make sure his home was hallowed, the other struggled up and wobbled away, to be chased for a few yards and lose part of his tail.

I got hold of my rooster and sponged off his head. I had never seen a cockfight before, or imagined one, or envisaged a future involving cockfighting. Now I knew I had a champ. Now I thought of the cocky roosters up and down the alley from our house.

Later in class I thought of the class of the Champ. A few more days and he'd be in condition again. What mattered spelling when the blood surged?

I caught him when he was healed. I tucked him under my arm. I sneaked down the alley, seeking an adversary. I came on one. I sneaked my fighter into the yard and lay concealed in his corner. He went out with great spirit. Victory took only minutes. I crawled inside, drew him to me and took him home.

He enjoyed fighting. He came to expect it. It got so that he would wait for me to pick him up and start for the arena. Always he came out best. Up and down the alley other roosters bore the marks of his beak and spur. Their owners couldn't understand.

And then one day he failed me. That day, without once showing fight, he ran and kept on running, kept on slamming into the fence while the other rooster chased and flailed him.

I carried the ex-champion home, sick at what I'd seen. I brooded. Not for a week did a return engagement come to mind—and this one on home grounds! I caught the new champ while the owners were away. I took him to the Silver-Laced arena, and there the old champ whipped the holy smoke out of him, and I was happy again.

We maintained our flock by setting hens on eggs the hens had laid and Champ had fertilized. Father feared the effects of inbreeding and eventually bought a new rooster, one with no class or spirit; and a great time was over.

I don't know what happened to the old bird. I suppose we ate him.

We didn't, however, eat one hen that misfortune overtook. She had got out of the barnyard and fallen into the privy.

Early one evening my brother, Chick, came in with the news. Slowly, as the problem presented itself, Father's face set. He'd been preparing his talk for the Bible class Sunday, and now he had to save from the pit a fool, though purebred, Silver-Laced Wyandotte. Inexpectation again. A confounded break in routine. He gave the case severe thought.

"We'll have to snare her," he said after a while.

He meant to use, we knew, a fishing pole and short length of copper wire with a small running noose in it. With such a contrivance, in the clear waters of Spring Creek and the Teton, we had learned to catch suckers and whitefish, though rarely the wily and muscular trout. You simply slipped the noose over the fish, cinched it tight with a quick jerk and heaved the catch out of the water and overhead onto the bank.

"Light the lantern," Father commanded. "Tie a piece of sash cord to the handle so we can lower it." With the air of a man beset but unbowed he went outside to rig up the tackle.

Chick readied the lantern. By that time Father was

waiting. With uncommon foresight he'd chosen a rather short pole because of the cramped space in the privy.

The privy was a two-holer. Led by Father, we marched to it single file. Through one hole I lowered the lantern. Father poked his pole down the other. There, wading around, was the hen, sure enough, though by this time she hardly looked like a Wyandotte, much less a Silver-Laced one.

"Hold the lantern still!" Father said guttily as the noose missed.

I was holding it still.

He maneuvered the snare with delicacy and slow guile, but he didn't deceive the hen. A hen outside an outhouse, without a snare approaching, still has a nervous head.

Father said, "Confound it!" With his knees on the floor and the bulge of his stomach pressed hard on the deck, he was getting uncomfortable and somewhat winded. It didn't improve his disposition to have Chick, an eager observer, breathing down his neck.

Now he said, "The devil!"

I suggested I have a try.

Nothing doing, confound it. He had set out to snare her himself, and snare her he would.

He gave the pole a sudden mighty jerk. The hen soared up and would have gone into orbit except for the ceiling. He brought her down to the floor where she flapped like a chicken with its head cut off. The head might as well have been. He had broken her neck.

There was a paralyzed, front-line moment.

Then I yanked the lantern aloft, and the three of us bulged the door frame as we burst away from the shrapnel, not without casualties.

We regrouped our forces outside. In the lantern's light Father's face bore a look of hard satisfaction. He had met the enemy and bested him cleanly, and what mattered a hen or our wounds?

With one exception Father went along patiently with the preachers assigned to our church. He even admired a couple of them. Others he liked and still others endured, I suppose out of belief in over-all benefit. The ones he admired, I recognize now, were those with the sense to feel a sense of disquiet at items of Methodist doctrine.

But for all his doubts about doctrine he must have enjoyed church, for duty alone seems hardly sufficient to account for his labors. He taught the Bible class for twenty-five years. Season on season, until the termination I'm coming to, he headed with scant help the annual fund-raising campaign. He sang in the choir. He rarely missed a function. The socials—we didn't call them sociables—that the Ladies' Industrial conducted were musts for all of us. And welcome ones, too.

The church would be good with the smells of stewed chicken and hot biscuits; the odors of mincemeat and pumpkin would be in the air, and of potatoes fresh-grown and butter fresh from a churn. The minister, down from his pulpit, had left his message behind, and the good ladies bustled, making sure that he and all hands got well fed. In remembrance the ladies were all warm and kind and full-bosomed and so assured the small fry, by unconscious connection, of plenty of chicken and trimmings.

There is a story, perhaps apocryphal and certainly never familiar to Father, about an early-day minister. Like many men of that time, the minister kept a cow, and his had recently freshened. One Sunday morning after he had put on his church garb it occurred to him he hadn't given the calf its lesson in relinquishing teats in favor of basin or bucket. He had time to do so before promoting the cause of the Lamb and so poured some milk out and went to the barn.

To wean a calf you dip your fingers in its drawn measure of milk and induce it to sample them and in the process tease its head down to the false source of supply.

This, with care for his cloth, the minister did. After some experimentation the calf raised its head, took a look at its trainer and thereupon sneezed mucus and milk on the Sabbath-day suit.

The preacher grabbed the calf by its ears. He thrust its head into the pail. "If it wasn't for Jesus Christ and my immortal soul," he said, "I'd ram your goddam head clear through this goddam bucket!" Father liked this minister.

It was the Reverend Mr. Smithers, as I'll call him, that he couldn't endure. Among Father's top abominations were, in his terms, humbugs and humbuggery. The words were expletives, severer than designations like blowhards and four-flushers, which he employed, too, though with no knowledge of the derivation of the latter.

And here, assigned to the Choteau Methodist Episcopal Church, came Mr. Smithers, a small, jolly, oily chap, full of good works, quick with the glad clap on the shoulder, who called saint and sinner brother and went about with sweet anointment. From his pulpit issued sugary inanities.

By George, a humbug! Father served notice he wouldn't lead again the church's annual campaign for funds.

Mr. Smithers wouldn't take no for an answer. He was the servant of the Lord, and God was with him. He didn't know Father.

With what civility he could muster, Father pleaded private pressures. Mr. Smithers put a small, warm arm across his back. He gave him an apostle's pat. "I know, Brother Guthrie," he said, smiling, "but your shoulders are broad."

"Yes, Brother Smithers," Father answered and used a word he rarely did. "My shoulders are broad, and your butt is narrow, but I believe I can kick it."

In speaking of my father I've been superficial and a good deal too gentle. I look back over the roll of the years and wonder, disposed now to forget his cruelties and remember his credits, though all of his children bear the scars of his savage unreason.

In the way of money a man more honest never lived. He strained that quality, I think in my adulthood, though my respect abides. Because he had recommended Montana second mortgages and kinsfolk back in Indiana had suffered as a consequence, he felt obliged to make up their losses, ranking that questionable debt above the needs of his immediate family. The times were lean when he was bank cashier. An occasional and slender source of income came to homesteaders from oil companies just then gambling on Montana. Men with land made him their agent, saying they would lease, say, for two bits an acre. When he got more, as sometimes he did, he paid them the total, rejecting the overage that other agents would have felt themselves entitled to. Once he had established himself in the community, no one ever questioned his integrity. Often he was asked to help settle estates and always did so for nothing, though heirs were willing to pay.

Though not a big man physically, he had courage that few men do. Teaching was a sissy occupation, or so some

thought when he arrived in town. He wrenched a quirt from
one of them, after a slash across the face, and put the run on
him. He once walked into the eye of a revolver, first pointed
at a friend of his, and won possession of it. No big-boy row-
dies in his school intimidated him. An old-time master, he
didn't hesitate to clobber them. Be it said for them, they
came to like him as a consequence. In later years more than
one has thanked me for his discipline and wished he were on
hand to thank. It seems strange in these days that parents
didn't protest. I can't recall that any ever did.

I must insert here, while admiring his brute courage,
that I count him part coward. To be sure, the physical setting of Choteau and Montana had much to do with his remaining where he was; yet another element was fear, the fear
of further challenge, of new responsibilities, of encounter
with more than local intellects. As a home-town performer he
excelled, but what of other stages? Outside the local, outside
the physical, he had little confidence and, unsure of himself,
stood solid and sullen against wider opportunity. With ugly
granite he hid trepidation.

But his high school, though small, ranked with the best
in Montana. He was not only a disciplinarian but also, and
more important, a true scholar. Latin, English, mathematics, history, the science of that time—he could teach
them all and teach them well. Subjects came to life under his
tutelage. Interests broadened. His advice gave depth and
direction to more lives than I can say. One of them was mine,
though it happened that I never was his classroom student.
The stimulus and guidance that I got from him I got at
home. I'm grateful for it. But for his interest in literature,
but for his profound attachment to nature and the West,
which took me into books and carried me afield to buffalo
wallows, birds' nests, landmarks and sites of old excitement

and made his loves my own, I doubt I would be writing now. Count under unearned blessings, the blessing of having or of having had parents both educated and aware.

He loved us, this I know, but devils dwelt in him, inexplicable and uncontainable. He was a man of vast impatience, of dark and instant angers. Stupidity, the unforeseen, chance variations and interruptions of plans and routines, God knows what—these fired his blood. Chick said later that, aroused, he had all the good will of a rattlesnake.

We had a one-eyed bird dog, Jimps. When I was old enough to ask, Father explained that as a pup she had been prone to range too far while hunting and, to teach her better, he'd dusted her with birdshot. One of the pellets, he said mildly, had chanced to strike her eye. Then I took his word for it. Now I know that fury pulled the trigger.

Later on, Jimps came in heat, and male dogs hung around the house. The sight of them filled Father with fierce embarrassment. In his mind, I'm sure, there was an association here with evil. Sex on his doorstep! One night during her season old Jimps clawed out of the screened-in back porch and "got stuck" in the garden. Father seized my boy's ball bat, marched out and clubbed her on the head. The blow burst her seeing eye.

And so he had to shoot her. I can see him again, slow with the shotgun, the demon in him overcome too late; and there sounded the reluctant shot, the thunder clap of destruction.

Years later I wrote a short story, *Ebbie*, drawing painfully on these memories. It frightened the editors of big and presumably sophisticated magazines, a couple of whom wrote me rather elaborate if unconvincing letters of rejection. One said that if his magazine were to publish it, there would have to appear in the same issue three or four brightside stories, and the total would violate the format. The little *Southwest Review* took it, though. It's now in several anthologies.

Old Fox roiled Father, too. Once, with three of us kids aboard bareback, Fox shied on entering the gate and spilled us all. Unhurt, we laughed until Father, a witness, seized a club and went to work.

Physically, Father wasn't violent with us children. As I remember, he struck me only once, and then not hard enough to hurt. Nor can I recall that he ever laid hands on the others. He didn't need to. His angry tones made stomachs crawl. His dark deportment weighed on our hearts. Always, it seems in memory, we walked on tiptoe, even Mother, fearful that some trifle would eclipse the sun that he could be. Even when we went on jaunts, to fishing holes or picnic grounds, we went gingerly, fearful that Father, a great man for shortcuts, would get lost or stalled, as he often did. In either case, he always spoiled the day for us.

When Chick and I were grown and gone, my young sister Jane had to deal alone with him except, of course, for Mother. In 1929, I think it was, I returned from Kentucky on vacation; and here was remembrance reenacted and magnified by the reduction of targets. Poor Janie. I took her to Lexington, where I had worked for three years, for her junior term in high school. She made straight A's there with ease. Afterwards she and Father got along better, if not well. She completed high school at Choteau while he was principal and would have been valedictorian had he let her be. Though proud of her grades, he reduced her a notch, saying that Lexington's Henry Clay High School, while it might be the best in that city, was not up to snuff.

In my late teens I defied Father absolutely and won my independence of his tantrums, and, as the years went on, he came to lean on me. For all his sins, I found that reversal sad and somewhat frightening, as any young man does when old supports give way and, standing alone and unsupported, he becomes supporter.

To the boyhood me it was Father, in himself, who gave meaning to the term "God-fearing," for he was God, whom no one understood and everyone, in recognition of his own ignorance, forgave. I catch his image across the years. I see a strong and handsome face and see myself trotting from the house to meet him when school is out, and I stand hesitant on the board walk, straining to determine whether his expression is benign or malignant; and as a man I know I own something of him and am not always proud of it.

Mother was no patsy. When she spoke, he heeded, if reluctantly. But controversy was not in her nature, nor did she want quarrels to take place in the presence of the children. At night she must have tried to reason with him, for she told me he never went to sleep without an apology for fractiousness. For her that was enough, or almost, for she loved him as he had no right to expect. And she used to explain to me, with the strain in her face showing as one of the scars he'd inflicted, that he came by his temper through the hot-tempered Paynes on his mother's side and forever fought to moderate it. A losing fight, I'd say now.

I do not know what furies rode him. Hot temper through heredity, really? Pure physical bile beyond control of will? Too much virility for the monogamy he practiced? So much early tragedy in the family? The haunting sense of doing poorly with the talents he'd been endowed with? I do not know.

Whatever hate I had for him I loved is gone. I feel sorrow; and when I cast back to him without casting farther, I see his smile and feel his hand kind on my shoulder and hear his cheerful voice; and we have a chaw of licorice and catch a trout or find an arrowhead and speculate about the men who lived before us.

I go to the family graveyard and read the inscription on a stone he put there after most of us were dead and he had come to live alone.

Warm summer sun,
Shine kindly here;
Warm southern wind,
Blow softly here;
Green sod above,
Lie light, lie light.
Good night, dear hearts,
Good night, good night.

It required the constitution of a crocodile, inside and out, to survive the domestic medical aids of my boyhood, and the indifference of ignorance and custom to endure without embarrassment the clothes we children wore.

"You feeling all right, Son?" Father would ask, looking at me with a combination of concern and irritation.

"All right," I would say with what assurance I could muster. An affirmative answer was better than his antidotes.

"He does look a little peaked," Mother would put in.

"Bilious!" Father would say. Bilious was one of his favorite diagnoses, perhaps because he was so often atrabilious.

They'd get the fever thermometer out then and pop it

in my mouth. There were few days when one or another of us youngsters wasn't having his temperature taken.

"Uh-huh," Father would report, squinting at the tattletale line of mercury. "Just as I thought. One hundred and two." His genuine solicitude was made more weighty by his dark air of triumph.

There was just one medicine for biliousness, and that was calomel, which I wouldn't recommend today for any of God's creatures, barring maybe a foundered horse or one that had just kicked me without cause. We took it, staggering, in staggered doses, a tablet every hour, I believe it was, until we were drained of all substance, including our offending livers. Within a week we usually managed to recover.

For lesser gastrointestinal disturbances there were lesser nostrums, all purges of course. Castoria, for instance, and, up the ladder in severity, castor oil and licorice powder, which the body rejected with some haste; but for honest-to-God action nothing equaled calomel.

No one has the croup any more. As a word for a cough and sore throat it has fallen from use in favor of strep, staph, virus and flu. We weren't so definitive. We had, and kept having, the croup. Our parents were prepared for it. In the medicine cabinet were swab sticks, cotton and a bottle of tincture of iron, there by grace of a medical science that thought painting the tonsils was the real ticket. For croup, that is, and for tonsillitis, which nearly equated. One coat of iron wasn't enough. That, so to speak, was merely the sizing. The number depended on the immediate project and might very well exhaust the bottle. I learned to paint my throat myself and did it every day one winter in California, where Father had sent Mother and us children in the hope that Baby John and I would grow less puny. For this faithful self-medication I was to get a dollar a week. That was the same sum Father paid the preacher, and I attended to my chore with such preacherish dedication that even today, if a doctor asks to see my throat, I can reveal my ulcer without benefit of tongue depressor.

Just for good measure, if the case appeared to call for it, Mother would prepare a throat poultice for night application. She'd line one of her old stockings with strips of bacon, shake lots of salt and pepper over it, and pin the stocking around the neck. The treatment left a grained band of red over the affected parts but, unlike others, did seem remedial, or so it seems now to have been.

There was asafoetida, that famous warder-off of germs. Each of us wore a little sack of it against his chest, suspended there by a necklace of store string. My parents were highly skeptical but yielded to our arguments that all the other kids in school had theirs. Were we to be freaks? I'd rather be a freak than sniff that stuff again. Thinking of it, I think of carrion and body waste but know I've missed the evil ingredient that made it more offensive than both combined. People must have tended to humanize germs those days; they thought no germ, however ill-disposed, would come within a whiff of such a stink.

As from forgotten croup we suffered from forgotten chilblains. When feet got cold and touched with frost, they itched and stung within the warmth of school and home, and who could manage phonics, much less fractions, when his mind was on his feet? The pupils from outlying farms and ranches, who came to class by horse or horse and buggy, had the harder time of it. The teacher sometimes sent them running barefoot through the snow. Snow was the remedy for chilblains and any kind of frostbite. On bitter days a bucket of it stood within the schoolhouse door, to be applied with vigor to ears and noses that showed white. Hair-of-the-dog principle, I suppose. Even my parents embraced it. Sometimes it wasn't until spring or even summer that our feet stopped hurting.

We used Vaseline or flour and water for our burns, cow's cream for sunburn, turpentine for cuts, liniment for aches and pains, kerosene and fine-toothed combs for head lice, by which we were humiliated once, and spiders' webs for warts. We rolled the webs into a ball, put the ball on the wart and touched a match to it. It burned like punk and, burning, made us dance. Afterwards, we ran a needle through the scorch of wart and pried it off with little pain.

Except for lumbago, which goes by different names now, Father was seldom indisposed. I can't remember that he ever took or had to take the remedies prescribed for us, though he would take quinine for a head cold, as we did too. It was just as effective as modern nostrums and in addition, as if in token of avail, set up a fine ringing in the ears.

None of us ever contracted thrush, but Father told me an old granny in southern Indiana divulged her secret cure to him. She took his infected baby brother behind the barn and to the baby's oral cavity applied a fresh horse ball. (His noun.) Antibiotic?

Mother underwent an operation for hernia in Indianapolis years ago but, saving that disorder, seemed never sick until at last cancer caught her up. Or if she was, she didn't let us know. We assumed she'd always be on hand to minister to us, without an ache or pain or fever of her own. Pregnant or just delivered of a baby, she was there for us; she was the impervious symbol of Home, Sweet Home.

Come September, when the first snow often fell, we donned long underwear, called union suits because tops and bottoms couldn't be divorced. We had a choice here. We could buy them with drop seats that buttoned and unbuttoned at the sides or with split seats that single buttons presumably sufficed for. In either case they were shapeless garments, made more shapeless by the wearing. One use, and they were butt-sprung, knee-sprung and ankle-sprung. It was the ankles that bothered me. No matter how carefully we lapped the flaccid fabric and smoothed our stockings over it, we looked trim only for an hour or so. Then the laps would loosen and the fabric climb and bunch above our shoes like bulged veins about to pop. That mortified me. More than once in school I made the signal for the toilet—one upheld finger for the kidneys, two for the bowels—just to remedy my varicosity. (I wonder why the teachers insisted on knowing whether their charges had to urinate or defecate, and do any still insist?)

Now if it happened, as it rarely did, that the pedal ends of underwear had stayed in place till bedtime, a careful but timesaving operation was in order. That was to remove stockings and underwear in combination without disturbing the adjustment that had served so well. A tricky thing, but if it worked then dressing in the morning was made quick and easy. Just pull underwear and stockings on together, again being careful, though.

Until we got a fixed bathtub that was lined with copper and often left the dark marks of corrosion on the skin, we bathed just once a week, a couple of us using, in order, the same water in the laundry tub. We must have become pretty dirty, but I wasn't conscious of it.

Between their clumsy underwear and shirts or blouses, pre-school and grade-school boys and girls, except for an overgrown boy or two who had graduated to long pants, wore Ferris waists—a name and designation almost unknown now. They buttoned up the front, if I remember right, and had a flock of other buttons on them, yet served a single purpose. Connected by garters, they held stockings up or, rather, kept them from complete collapse. It was a happy day for us when Mother discovered Fay stockings. The fronts of these extended up and buttoned directly to the waist. No more garters.

It wasn't until the eighth grade or the first year of high school that most boys got long pants. Until then we had worn knickerbockers. The change was as momentous as is a modern girl's first dance formal, though we carried it off with less grace. We stood around sheepishly, proud yet self-conscious, flinching at the barbs of those who'd been transformed before. I showed up at a dance in my first long trousers, complete with matching Norfolk jacket, and ran away when an older boy said he bet I still was wearing stockings and not manly socks. I was.

Little boys wore baggy, short-cut pants with elastic at the knees or closer-fitting ones likewise cut short. Both buttoned at the side. The front was unbroken except for a little slit referred to as the pee-hole. Strategically located, it had an inside flap or valve to cover up the vent when it was not in use. Considering the heavy clothes we wore, I wonder how we small ones managed.

Father was a neat and dignified dresser, always shaved, always clad with clean, pressed trousers, vest and coat, always shod with shoes which, if sometimes old, were shined. I never saw him on the street without a necktie. And now he had bought a new suit!

It happened at the time that George Jackson and I had come into possession of a runty pointer pup. It made up, in brains and willingness, for its want of size, and George and I were mighty proud. In true partnership he took care of the dog one week, I the next. It was my week when disaster fell.

Dad had hung his new vest on a chair. Mother would have put it away, but she was out of town. The pup curled up close to the stove, and we all went to bed.

I was first up, being stoker of the fires, and there was Father's vest without a button on it. The dog had chewed them all off and apparently consumed them, for not a button or a piece of one was to be found anywhere.

I got the dog out of the house. I ran with him to the home of George Jackson, who had to be awakened. I told George the frightful news and left the dog there.

Father was almost dressed when I got back to the house. He put on the vest and tried to button it. His face hardened as he made his deduction. "Where's that dog!" he said in tones that made my stomach knot.

"I let him out."

"All right," he said. "Never let him back!"

Later on the dog was poisoned. I don't know who did it, but I know it wasn't Father. In one of his black and sudden rages he might have clubbed the dog to death, but the premeditation of the poisoner was not in him.

Before the dog's death he began to think the thing was pretty funny, especially after Mother had returned and sewed new buttons on his vest.

4

It was taken for granted in my family that we young-sters would go to college. I can't recall that we ever debated the subject. On one occasion only did we come close to a controversy. With that juvenile resentment that splays out in all directions, I had been complaining about high school. I hated the necessity of attending, hated the burden of home-work, thought some of my teachers were stupid. Father listened with notable patience. Then he put aside the book he had been reading.

"All right," he said. "You don't have to go to school. You can quit tomorrow. With your training I'm sure you can get a job as a printer. Moreover, you know a good deal about ranch work. You've handled horses, put up hay, harvested wheat, tended sheep, tied fleeces and all that. Maybe we'll be able to manage a small start for you as a rancher."

His statement was so mild, so unexpected, so free of outward reservation that I stood disarmed and dismayed and then hastened to my books. I didn't want to be a printer or a rancher. I wanted to put words on paper. It was some years before I suspected Father of having been sly.

We considered higher schools and decided, for no remembered reasons, that the University of Washington at Seattle was the place for me. So in the fall of 1919 we set out by car on the twenty-mile trip to Dutton, Montana, then a flag stop for the Great Northern's Oriental Limited. With my parents and me went a friend a few years my senior, who proposed to resume his once-forsaken studies.

As the old Dodge rattled over the gravel road, Mother sang "God Will Take Care of You" with what must have been a frail assurance. The last of belief. The irreducible residue of hope in heavenly benevolence.

The train stopped on signal. Mother gave me a last embrace. Father and I shook hands like men, neither of us looking at the other for fear of being undone. My friend and I boarded. And I was frightened already and homesick, feeling empty and heavy with emptiness.

High school had been a kind of cozy fun and Choteau the center of my universe. I knew everyone in town. I had been a better than medium-sized frog there, and the puddle was big enough. I was on the basketball team. I could polevault better than most. Summertimes I pitched for the town baseball team. At none of these things was I ever really good, just good enough in the absence of more candidates to make the varsity. I made money after hours at the *Acantha* and forthwith spent it—which no doubt helped explain my stature in the puddle. My grades were always respectable. And I

had a girl, a good and pretty girl, and enjoyed my classmates' envy.

Then to be cast in Seattle's sea!

The city was too big for me. So was the university. I
was always alien there, a country boy unused to crowds, unaccustomed to procedures and too shy to inquire. Out of
trepidation and defensive pride I pretended I had been
around and sometimes was exposed.

Most of all I disliked the climate. Days on end of rain
and cloudy skies, and where the sun was was a guess. With a
.22 rifle, using shorts, I could have punctured the overhang.
I knew the Montana sky, the wide, deep and azure sky, seldom gray, where the sun came up in a burst of glory and
sailed serene and nestled at dusk in the arms of the western
Rockies. There was freedom. There the spirit reached up and
out, liberated and unlimited. Beyond the eye's reach there
was promise.

I endured my nine months in Seattle, vowing never to go
back.

The next year I transferred to the University of Montana at Missoula, where I spent three school years and won a
degree as a major in journalism.

Journalism, we had agreed, seemed a likely choice for
one who wanted to write. Perhaps Father's experience as a
country editor was a factor. It must have been: my brother
and sister majored in the same field later on.

As of that time the selection was a happy one. Arthur L.
Stone, the dean of the school, was an experienced newspaper-
man, to be sure, but he was first of all a kindly philosopher.
There were few "must" courses in the theory and practice of
newspapermaking. He wanted us to have the backgrounds of
English, history, ethics, political science.

Nowadays, though liberalizing influences are at work, a

major often allows so little time for other studies that the graduate, deep in his trench, cannot see the skyline. One meets them all too often—holders of degrees in engineering, forestry, medicine, and, in particular, education, who are illiterates in subjects other than their own and sometimes even then.

Missoula was a happier place, closer to home, clearer-skyed, far smaller in total population and student enrollment than Seattle. Most of my classmates were people of my kind—which is to say they came from small towns, too, and were ignorant of the urbanity that I stood in awe of, yet wished to have. I joined a fraternity, with less than a whole heart, and became its president, though a more important function was to help keep the house grade average up. Football players were our prize members then.

If grades are an index, I did well. Sometimes I think I was too quick to learn, for the quick learner is a quick forgetter, and many a man who had to plug for merely passing grades retains more than the classmate who achieved easy A's.

I don't know what I learned in college. To save me, I couldn't now approach a simple problem in trigonometry. I can't read even easy French, though once I read French novels with rare recourse to a dictionary. Zoology, logic, anthropology, medieval history—where are they now?

Just as lost to mind are the teachers that I had. I can name but five or six, and two of them, the best ones, graveled me. One got fired a few years afterwards, ostensibly because he let "son of a bitch" be printed in the campus literary magazine. Later on, after he had made a shining reputation at Dartmouth, I discovered in what debt I was to him and thought of his detractors in the plural of the term he had approved.

Yet changes occurred in me, through contacts, reading and lectures dull and bright. Though I wasn't ready to embrace the whole idea of human brotherhood and so renounce preferred position, I remembered with misgivings in my senior year an answer given two years earlier. An instructor of forgotten name had asked his students to list their prejudices. I couldn't think of one and wrote down "None." No prejudices, but we didn't want a Jew in the fraternity and were careful about that. There was only one Negro on campus, a fine boy, too, as all admitted, but he was a Negro. It was fortunate we had no Indians in the student body. Everyone knew about Indians. No prejudices, just a normal capacity for realism.

One dislike, which professional men at arms and apoplectic patriots will count as prejudice or worse, developed early and is still in my gizzard: that was a dislike of the military, to which I had two years' exposure as an unwilling member of the Reserve Officers' Training Corps. Granted unhappily that we need him, the man on horseback along with his obedient underlings is at odds with American tradition. Who makes a career of Army, Navy or Air Force? Not men, I think, who deeply feel in blood and bone the commonality of man.

The accident of birth date kept me from two world wars—but I'd have been a doubtful asset anyhow. Too independent and perhaps too fearful. And too reluctant to kill. In extremity I suppose that I would shoot a man, but a sorry memory would abide. It can and will be argued that it's a lucky thing there weren't and aren't more of my kind.

Gone by the time I graduated was the last shred of belief in supernatural religion. In its place was a vehement rejection that, if less vocal now, yields not an inch to argument. Gone was complacency about our social order. I became a liberal, if that word has meaning any more. "Rebel" may be better. In that cast of mind in years succeeding, I voted once for Bob LaFollette and twice for Norman Thomas. I wouldn't do so now, but they made sense to me then. My rebelliousness didn't carry me on to communism. Hating all police states, I never wanted any part of it, and today am put out by the glad reception given those who, once blind, tardily have come to see.

I'm glad I took off from the hallowed ground of politics and economics, and I would argue, though not because my case is proof, that such youthful takings-off are good. Young people ought to soar. Most of them will settle soon enough and be the better for their flights.

I had been a believer and, through unexamined family background, a conservative, and I emerged from college an agnostic and a liberal. I suppose reading was the first cause, though my reading was spotty, partly because of a lack of continuity in English courses, partly because I had no program of my own and chose books hit or miss. To this day, though I've read much, my areas of total ignorance embarrass me. *Main Street*, just out, unsettled yet delighted me, and I thought Sinclair Lewis great. Henry Mencken gave me exultant pause, though at first I sided with his adversary, Stuart Pratt Sherman. Hardy awakened me to universal tragedy, and for years I walked in his dark shadow and to some extent still do. The naturalist John Burroughs, in prose an echo of Walt Whitman, was a comfort. I had to be told by a professor that one reason for my liking was that his language was so spare; but I liked nature, too, and, forsaking Methodism, half-embraced a pantheistic faith and found defense against despair in declarations like "The longer I live the more my mind dwells on the beauty and the wonder of the world." Thackeray, Voltaire, Anatole France,

H. G. Wells, Theodore Dreiser—these and others played some part in my shaping. From Swinburne and his now-seen as too-facile lines, I got a pleasant melancholy and couldn't comprehend then what Father found in Frost.

Most of the influential writers mentioned here, along with numerous and unmentioned others, I can't read any more; and I think it forlorn, with few exceptions, for anyone after the passage of years to reach back in an attempt to recapture old and great impressions. The same response no longer is in us. We see our youth, but as strangers to it; and the writings that awakened and exalted and depressed and helped to mold us seem dull and unprofitable.

I may be too nearly absolute. A penalty of authorship is the restriction of range as a reader. The present-day author, if he works at his craft, if he comes to some understanding of what is really good prose in fiction or fact, finds fewer and fewer books that enthrall him. For myself I'll never read again a line of Sinclair Lewis. Reaching back once, I discovered I couldn't go on with *Tess of the D'Urbervilles*, under whose cloud I had lived for so long. Dreiser, for all his power, is too awkward to take. Afraid of disappointment, I haven't reread Frank Norris, much as I used to like him. Shaw is too wordy. Swinburne is too easily expert, Mencken too showy, Wolfe too much woe-is-me. Of the authors who used to engage me I find Conrad and his smoky prose perhaps the most rewarding now.

Reviewing my changed and changing judgments, I keep returning to Alfred North Whitehead, the philosopher, in whose words I find challenge and faith and respect for true craftsmen of whatever kind. He wrote:

> The sense of style is an aesthetic sense, based on admiration for the direct attainment of a foreseen end, simply and without waste. Style in art, style in literature,

style in science, style in logic, style in practical execution, have fundamentally the same qualities, namely attainment and restraint. The love of a subject, where it is not the sleepy pleasure of pacing a mental quarterdeck, is the love of style as manifested in that study . . . style, in its finest sense, is the last acquirement of the educated mind; it is also the most useful. It pervades the whole being . . . style is the ultimate morality of mind.

In my sophomore year I discovered the girl that I married—but "discovered" is hardly the word, for I had known her since she was a wet-pantied nuisance toddling after us older children. She dawned on me! She was only fifteen at the time I took fresh inventory, but the years had made an astonishing difference. I felt a little sheepish—I, a college man, courting a virtual beginner in my old town high school. I courted her nonetheless, and for nine full years, by letter and wire and telephone and unhappily infrequent encounters. Her final consent I attribute to attrition. Marrying her, I became a member of her family and a dear and close friend of her father, Tom Larson, an old-timer whose wit and wisdom have often served me in my writing.

In my senior year a not-so-happy thing occurred. I fell victim to a neurosis, one that still haunts me, though not so much these days, one that must have been seeded in my system years before. Called on to read or speak before a crowd or class or a company of even three or four, I got terrified, became hysterical. My face worked and my knees shook. My voice trembled and gave out. I could not understand why. Later I read all the Freud and Jung I could find, seeking knowledge of myself, and wound up at a point at which I disliked to enter a store to buy a pair of socks unless I knew the clerk well. Complete self-effacement, that was for me. So much had I acquired from fundamentalist Christianity. So much for having been a good boy whose thoughts and dreams and nightmare vice proved I was unlike the righteous lot, a sinner born in sin. I had rejected primitivism long since, but its gifts stayed on.

The chairman of the Rhodes Scholarship Committee for our district, unaware of my infirmity, suggested pointedly that I apply. I didn't. I suppose I was too frightened, but I told myself that I had had enough of school and hungered for real life. In the spring of 1923, enamored, neurotic and graduated, I set forth in search of it, full of ambition—and apprehension.

Two years and more passed before I went to work for a newspaper. I didn't want a place in Montana, for the dailies were small, limited in opportunity and, save for two or three, owned by the Anaconda Copper Company and for the most part operated with small disguise as company organs. They weren't for me.

I wasn't eager, anyhow, to strike out in that summer after graduation. My girl was in town. I enjoyed—and always have—the company of my brother, Chick, a boy both kind and witty. I had a half-paternal, wholly loving regard for my sister, Janie, then hardly out of tothood, feeling with some right that I'd almost reared her. There were Mother and Father.

Soon enough fall would come around. When it did, I'd head south for old Mexico in company with Al Dalby, my former classmate at the University of Washington. Al had got to be editor of the *Choteau Acantha* and on invitation moved into the family home, where he became one of us. But a restlessness was in him. He had a brother in Sonora, the owner of a rice and wheat ranch, who'd have work for us if we delayed our trip a while. Here, now, was summer, Montana summer, the long, rich days, the dear associations under friendly skies, the time of not wanting things ever to change. Could life be so good again? I went to work with a haying crew on a ranch not far from town.

I had encountered Al first on a sheep ranch where, as an itinerant worker, he had asked for a job and been given the duty of driving the gut wagon—a wagon so-called because it brought from the range to the shed lambs freshly delivered and ewes stringing afterbirth. Though he was ten years and more my senior we struck up a friendship at once. He had attended Iowa State College at Ames but quit for some reason, financial, I think. Since then he had roamed, working in harvest and hay fields, sweating and freezing on ranches, doing the rough chores that offered themselves, though he had a mind and a curiosity and a wide reading knowledge that argued for more than the employment of muscle. Among men doing similar work he was a sport. Make it an anomaly: he wasn't sporty.

Al was a big man and had the big man's amiable tolerance—the unspoken but manifested apology for undue and accidental advantage. He was ugly, too, until you got to know him, ugly and made uglier later by a mishap that almost sheared off the tip of his nose. Driving home with companions from a country dance one night, he tried a short cut home over a shallow lake presumably frozen solid and ran into open water and got thrown through the windshield. Stitched back by some sutural inexpert, the nose end made a poor joint with the bridge. He had a big, broad, fighter-like face already, and the misfit dab of flesh completed an impression of the dazed and retired pugilist. Maybe an Englishman, name lost to memory, described him better in describing the appearance of another. He wrote of his man—I'm paraphrasing—that he wore a look of mild astonishment, like that of an artificially inseminated cow. No matter. Al was Al, a good man all the way. He died more than ten years ago, but I call him back, not as ex-pugilist or wondering cow, but as the person of parts he was.

Fall came. We said goodbye. Janie clung to me, crying, pleading that I not leave. Al had tears in his eyes. I couldn't see. We stumbled into Al's Model T, name of Lizzie, and set off down the gravel road. Goodbye. Goodbye to girl and family and the time that shouldn't end. Goodbye, Montana, and all of that. We got to go to Mexico!

Al had paid a hundred and fifty dollars for Lizzie and thought he'd struck a bargain. He was to lose that conviction fast. We weren't out of Montana before the brake went out, then the reverse that could be used as a brake, then the clutch that, if it worked, at least could slow you down some. We had new linings put in at Dillon, Montana. On once more, and soon the bands wore bare again. Eight dollars for each resole job, as I remember. Would our meager funds suffice?

We slept outside, a time or two in what could have been called jungles except that fellow denizens had transportation about like ours. We quarreled, Al and I, hot with that senseless hate that outward circumstances can kindle in affection. For a day we didn't speak. New linings for our brake and gears in Wyoming, Utah, Arizona.

We were going down the long, long switchback hill to Jerome, Arizona, where Al's uncle lived, when *everything* went out—brake, reverse, clutch and emergency.

Al was driving. He hollered, "Whoa!," and, receiving no response, brought Lizzie up against a boulder the size of a country courthouse. Not too much damage. For all her infirmities Lizzie had the constitution of a widow in a rest home. Nogales was our next stop, if we didn't have to stop sooner.

Somewhere between Phoenix and Tucson we picked up a thumber, a scarecrow man who lived by selling postcards with illustrations and bits of verse that came from his own hand and head. Ten cents each. When we dropped him off he left as payment for his lift the card that he liked best. It read:

Don't enter a town
Appearing a clown
With lip hanging down
Producing a frown.

There was more to his poem than those four lines, but they alone were abundant payment for his ride.

At Nogales we sold Lizzie. She had just been shod again and maybe was good for another three hundred miles before she called for help. We took the train to Cajeme, Sonora, where Al's brother was to meet us.

He was there, sun-helmeted, and put us in his car and drove through the mesquite to his place, which he or someone had exuberantly named the Hacienda Realidad. It stood on the bank of a canal that was a part of the irrigation system

from the Yaqui River that John Hays Hammond had arranged. Along the way we passed a dead horse, still saddled
and bridled. A Mexican troublemaker, it appeared, had been
fleeing from federal pursuers, who first shot the horse and
then the man, who'd tried to get away on foot. Casual incident, to be dismissed.

In the yard of the hacienda a little Mexican boy stood
naked, eating, tail first, an iguana, or wood lizard, an ugly,
spiked and crested thing, vestigial remnant of extinct and
ancient horrors. Dayton—that was Al's brother's name—
said the roasted flesh was fine.

Before he took us into the house, he cautioned us, pointing to the outdoor privy. In preparation for a sitting we had
better take a big fistful of old newspaper and rub it well
around the seat's unseen bottom side, thus dislodging chance
centipedes or scorpions. To one who disliked bugs unarmed
or armed, the warning was no help to regularity.

Random recollections, these. Incidentals. Small memories that stick while others stray. But I remember the poverty of the peons, who worked for a peso and a half a day
and of necessity had to do most of their trading at the
rancho commissary, where prices were jacked up. Matter of
custom. Maybe a matter of Yanqui survival. I didn't and
don't blame Dayton much. Who has a right to sit in judgment but one who has full evidence? I remember the shriveled, black and fly-blown meat that traveling butchers
brought to the doors of the airless adobes. The peons didn't
want air. With hats or whatever they promptly plugged
holes left for ventilation. And meat was meat. They bought
what they could without criticism and digested it without
untoward results. I remember the quail-hunting in the mesquite, the dove-hunting along fields of rice, the duck-hunting
on lagoon and canal. I remember the simple Mexicans' cheer-

ing when with a shotgun I brought down a duck, cheering because of the belief, held by American Indians before them, that a gun fired but one bit of lead and so only a deadeye could fell a bird on the wing. There were the night songs when the tired workers gathered on the bank of the ditch, the wistful, minor-keyed songs that sounded sad for the singers and sad for the world and made me ache for my girl, who hadn't written in two or three weeks.

The rice was right to be cut. We handled the binders, Al and I, seeing to the platform canvases, the elevators, the binding twine that had to be rather intricately threaded, the oiling of parts under friction. The peons knew nothing of any of this. They were as likely to oil the tongue of a binder as to put oil on a gear. So they shocked and weather-capped the bundles. One to each binder, they drove the double-span, eight-runty-animal teams that pulled the binders along, directing the course from a seat on one of the wheelers. They did so, all of them in whatever capacity, with the utmost good humor. Hearing them laugh, I wondered about the night songs.

There came the time to leave. The rice was cut. The wheat that would follow wouldn't be ripe for a long time. The odd jobs had been done. Al and I took off for Los Angeles, there to find the newspaper work we were meant for.

It would have been hard to find a harder time than we found in California in 1923 and 1924. The state—and for all that I knew, the whole nation—was in what is currently called a recession, or perhaps a real depression. We didn't use those terms. "Gross national product" hadn't emerged from the brooding brains of economists struggling with the English language. We knew only that *we* were depressed— and more depressed, as seekers of newspaper jobs, because

Cornelius Vanderbilt's Los Angeles tabloid had recently folded. Newspapermen with big-time experience were driving laundry trucks.

As our slender funds diminished, we rode the grub line, thankful for the generosity of old friends not much better off than we were. I hocked a fine, almost-new shotgun for fifteen dollars and never saw it again.

We went to Fresno. No work there either. For two or three nights we slept on park benches and were awakened early by an officer who used his billy on the worn soles of our shoes. I had my mother's check for fifty dollars in my pocket but wouldn't cash it. My parents had done enough for me. Let the copper use his club.

We beat our way to Oakland and there, through gyp employment agencies, found jobs. Al went to Petaluma, then and now known as "the world's egg basket." I visited him once. He had to water, feed and herd some several thousand Giant Pekin ducks that would go later to the San Francisco Chinese market. At sunset on the day of my visit he started hazing them toward overnight sheds half a mile or so away. Of necessity we traveled behind them, though that position was woeful with our inadequate equipment. Driving ducks, which somehow gain weight despite their ever-busy bowels, a man should wear gum boots.

I worked successively at two jobs. The first was with Western Electric at Emeryville just outside of Oakland. By report the outfit had a cost-plus contract with some other outfit—which accounted for its hiring more men than it needed. But because inspectors made their rounds we workers had to appear busy even when there was nothing to do, nothing even that the foremen could suggest. I never have worked harder than in that pretense of work and count it to my credit that I finally found an out. Stored in a neglected

corner was a high pile of sacks. I napped there safely, a plus
for Western.

Worn out with pretense, so well-napped I couldn't nap,
I went to work for a chain grocery, where I learned that
honesty, well advertised, was the best policy, and what customer, asking for veal liver, could distinguish it from pork?
Honest and gainful occupation, since the tongue could never
tell and pork was cheaper to the chain. With the store closed
and shuttered for the night, the fresh-vegetable manager
planted his fatigued asparagus in wet sawdust. Next morning the spears looked somewhat freshened and weighed more
than the night before.

The hours were long, the floors concrete. Hustling for
ten or twelve or fourteen hours a day on those ungiving
footings, I developed what a horseman might have called
bucked shins. For twenty-five dollars a week I had knotted
calf and thigh. It was a happy day when Montana called me
back.

I seldom saw Al thereafter and can't report on him in
detail, though we kept in uneven touch. He married, sired
children, edited a Fallon, Nevada, newspaper and became a
figure in the political affairs of county and state. Memory is
uncertain as to sequence and specifics, but from the mists he
comes to me with his smile and mutilated nose and gentle yet
firm character.

I had money enough for coach fare to Montana and
some dollars more. A coming-home gift for Mother then,
necessarily modest but thoughtful; I remembered from
our earlier stay in California how she enjoyed the small,
white sugar grapes that were not on sale at home. I bought a
thirty-five-cent basket.

I arrived at the station with the basket and my modest
luggage—and found that the train I wanted was all-

Pullman into Butte! I fumbled with my money. There was more than enough: one dime and one nickel more. Three candy bars for two days.

From Great Falls I took the local train that went to Choteau and beyond. I couldn't wait for the wheels to roll the miles. Through the open window of the coach I counted jackrabbits and telephone poles and got cinders in my eyes. With the pulsing eagerness that age diminishes, I thought how good, how good, how good, if only time would pass! The conductor, an old school friend of mine, stopped the train a mile beyond the town, opposite the family home about two hundred yards away. I thanked him and jumped off and stumbled down the grade and ran across a known field, past a clump of chokecherry bushes whose fruits I had enjoyed, over the now-paved highway, on toward home, with nothing in my pockets but with a heart high in my chest and, in my hand, a small basketful of grapes.

My job, a temporary one, had been offered by the local branch of the United States Forest Service, which was charged with the task of taking the decennial agricultural census.

As a census-taker I had to get around to places accessible by car and others difficult to reach on wheels in good weather and impossible in bad, and so I bought a used machine on tick and rented a spooky little gray filly. It was her practice, I learned later, to wheel around and jump back over the wire gates I had led her through and closed behind her. I never broke her of that determination: I just thwarted her. By leading her twenty-five or thirty yards beyond a gate, I could swing on and swerve her before she leaped the wires.

No matter her contrariness, I had to have her. Winter

came early and bitter. We broke through snow that no car could have run and survived frost and blizzards that would have immobilized the best of motors. In weather thirty degrees and more below zero we made out, thanks to that fool filly's stamina and the heavy underwear, the heavy shirt and pants and chaps and mackinaw and mitts and ear-flapped cap and overshoes that kept me just above the freezing point.

The ranchers generally were kind and generous, refusing to take pay for putting me up though they knew the government would foot the tab; but some were suspicious, not of me but of the undertaking, thinking, perhaps out of Nonpartisan League persuasion, that whatever advantages accrued would accrue to Wall Street.

Several ranchers advised me not to visit another, who lived alone and sequestered high in the hills. This man was crazy. He was known to burn the haystacks of those he disliked. He had shot at people with the rifle that he always had in hand. Stay away!

I had no firearm. For lack of one I put some rocks the size of goose eggs in my pockets and, feeling like David, knocked at his door. He wasn't in the house, but as I turned away I saw him coming through the pines. I saw the rifle, too, cradled in one arm. With my fingers tight on a pocketed stone, I greeted him and said why I was there.

Why, sure, he answered. Come on in. But before getting down to business he must show me a swan that he'd just shot and mounted. He led me into the house. The swan sat in a clothes basket filled with hay, its feathers bloody and its head arched high by means of a wire strung through its gullet. It would be stinking pretty soon. He asked me what I thought of it. What did I think of the work of a man with absolutely no training in taxidermy? I thought very well of it indeed. Then, pleased, he answered the questionnaire and begged me not to leave so soon. It wasn't every day that he got to talk to a man who could appreciate interests beyond the ordinary.

He was crazy, I suppose, but it was not his craziness that rode with me as I rode on.

At another ranch, a small and patently poor one, I found the housewife and three youngsters. Her man would be in soon, she said. Make myself comfortable in the seat he'd fashioned from a box. It was about the only place to sit if one ruled out a baby's highchair, presently unoccupied. The rightful tenant of it was toddling about, in diapers that ought to have been changed day before yesterday.

As morning wore toward noon, the woman took a moldering piece of meat from a shelf, put it on the seat of the highchair and proceeded to cut it up. Then she asked me if I wouldn't stay for a bite.

At still another place where I called before the start of winter, I took dinner with a family that had no more to deck the table with than hot and pithy radishes and bread and butter. No pay, thank you. It was enough to have my company.

Hard times in Montana. Lonely people. No radios for most folk and little mail. Every thought known in wife's or husband's head and so no need to say it. Every feature known and every habit, until the very knowing must have come to border on annoyance, and even sleep could hardly knit the sleeve of care.

One night a co-worker and I holed up in a hotel in the small town of Augusta. The mercury stood—or sat—at thirty-five below. A little stove heated the small lobby of the hotel. The two elderly lady proprietors had to hover close to it to keep their old flesh from freezing.

There was a dance in town that night, regardless, and quite a little crowd of men in the pool hall where a five-foot barber plied his trade. Flasks of moonshine were passing pretty freely.

We went on to the dance, and others came in, breathing white, as the chill music sounded along the chill street. After watching a while, we returned to the hotel and trembled into our frigid double bed and went to sleep.

At three o'clock in the morning, that hour of no courage, Bill shook me. "What's that? What's that?" he whispered. "What's that?"

From the room next to ours came the wild barking of a dog, then a wild pounding, then the barking again.

"Crazy!" Bill said. "Someone. Something. Listen!"

"We got to see," I whispered. "Can't stand to lie here listening."

"No! Sneak past the door and go downstairs. Talk to the ladies."

The ladies, in nightdresses, cowered by the stove. It was Shorty, the barber, they said. Drunk. He'd gone to his room drunk.

"No!" they beseeched me. "Don't go up there! Don't dare go up! He's got a rifle. He'll shoot."

I went to rout out the deputy sheriff. Bill stayed on as guard. The deputy lived alone in a log cabin. He didn't want to let me in. I told him the story. "Christ!" he said. "Crazy fool!" With no haste and less appetite he began pulling his pants over the long drawers he'd slept in. Dressed, he strapped a revolver around him, and we walked back to the hotel through the cold and crystal night.

Nothing had changed. The ladies were still cowering. Bill stood as the uncertain protector. And from above, as if almost upon us, came the same wild racket.

The deputy listened. "Crazy, all right," he announced. "Dangerous, too. I seen him before with a skinful of booze. Light us a lamp."

Somehow I found the lamp in my hand. Somehow I found myself leading the procession upstairs. Right behind me came the deputy, his six-gun in hand. I took it for granted he would take over when the chips were down.

We stood a minute outside the door. It sounded like a wolf with a tom-tom inside. Then the deputy slid his hand under my elbow, turned the knob, flung the door open and gave me a push. I made a splendid if unsteady target.

The rest is anticlimax. Shorty had come home too drunk to get into bed. In that icy room he had fallen face down on the floor. As we burst in upon him, he reared like a seal and howled like a hurt dog. Then he let himself down and hammered his face on the planking. Unconscious protest, nature's protest, at freezing to death.

We hoisted him up on his bed and covered him. He hadn't much skin left from temple to chin.

I didn't go back to see how he'd fared. My work took me elsewhere, and, when it was done, I set off for Attica, New York, there to work for an uncle and cousin who, under the name of the Thomas-Boyce Feed Company, milled and mixed rations for cows, horses and chickens.

My position, if not my wage, was elevated by my relatives. I wrote direct-mail advertising, visited small New York and Pennsylvania towns in the unfamiliar role of salesman and at times managed the retail store in Attica that the firm kept open as an adjunct.

Though not in the work I wanted, I wasn't unhappy, not even in the realization that I lacked a drummer's crust. I still thought of time as an everlasting credit and enjoyed my days. The small-town and country people of New York met me with an open, unfeigned friendliness such as I'd seldom known and have encountered seldom since.

Then one night the mill burned, from tall top to bottom level. It was an antiquated, shaky, ever-dusty structure, a poor bargain at whatever price, and the wonder was that it had stood so long. Starting high above, the fire burned downwards, and there was much talk the next day about the thousands of dead rats that lay about. Descending as the fire forced them to, they had run from the last retreat of the first floor and been fried outside by the heat from above.

I had more urgent considerations. Where was I to go, and how was I to get there? I had only a few dollars in my pocket, and the company wasn't going to rebuild.

I went to the Bank of Attica and talked to the cashier, an old-time gentleman with an interest in books and particularly in the works and life of Elbert Hubbard, the sage of nearby East Aurora. He greeted me warmly, thinking perhaps I wanted to talk authors again, but his manner changed not at all when I said I had to have money. Further, I wouldn't ask anyone to co-sign my note, and, still further, I didn't know where I was going. Maybe to Columbus, Ohio, where there was some promise of a public-relations post with a bank. Maybe to New Orleans, which I'd always wanted to visit. Maybe to Lexington, Kentucky, where my father's brother was sounding out the possibility of a newspaper job.

He listened, nodding, asked how much I thought I would need and, nodding again, brought out a blank note. He filled it in for $300, and I signed it, trembling.

The man's name was B. T. Sands, and I suppose he is dead and the time is too late to offer the full thanks that I should have, both then and later. Young people take acts of assistance and faith as matters of course. Thanks come from the old, addressed to the graveyard.

Within a few days I used part of the $300 for a train ticket for Lexington, where my uncle had been told I could start as a cub for the *Lexington Leader*. That was in July of 1926, and I was twenty-five. In Kentucky I began what career lay before me—and there I met Mary Lizzie.

6

I got the address from the Y.M.C.A. It was listed along with others where rooms might be had. The landlord, said the man at the desk, with Y.M.C.A. innocence, was a widow who needed tenants badly.

It went against my lingering Methodist conscience to consider possibilities, yet I did and, of course, went to the home of the widow first.

From the bus stop two blocks away from the address I walked up a decaying, narrow street, flanked by front-porched houses erected long ago. The neighborhood, if not ominous, still was not inviting, and I had about decided against any such location when the given number stared at me. All right. Since I had come this far, I might as well go see.

The house was two-storied, brick, old-fashioned, roofed with shingles of slate. The doorbell was manually operated. It churred to my pull, and I heard the sound of rather ponderous movement. Presently the door opened, and my illicit thoughts fell broken-winged, for there stood Mrs. Mary Elizabeth Keating.

She struck me as old. In one's twenties and or even thirties anyone of sixty is elderly. In the forties one extends the range and in the fifties extends it further still. Age depends on where you are. But she was old to my young eyes, and overweight besides. Her hair was fine and white but could stand combing, her nose a little red. On it was perched, somewhat awry, a pair of rimless glasses with thick lenses. When she looked through instead of over them, her eyes swam. I was too green to note, beyond these surfaces, how fine a face she had.

She spoke in the softest of unfamiliar Southern voices, "Good evenin'."

It wasn't evening to me. It was afternoon.

I told her why I had come and she nodded and said she would be glad to take ca'e of me and jes' hoped I'd like it heah. On the way through the dining room, before proceeding to a kitchen hallway which opened to an enclosed staircase leading upwards, she introduced me to an old friend of hers, a visitor from Bardstown, where both had been born. The visitor looked old, so old she had to use strips of adhesive tape to hold open her ancient eyes. Unknown to me, both were a little tipsy.

Mrs. Keating led me up the steep, dark steps, saying as she puffed up the treads that I could have either of the two rooms that composed the second story, for right now she had no tenants.

The rooms, though clean, were shabby. Beneath their

coverings, the mattresses looked lumpy. Heat came in either case from an open gas grate. The only bathroom was downstairs.

Out of politeness I told her I'd think about it, that I had two more places to inspect. I preceded her downstairs.

At the front door, her eyes crowding the lenses that she looked through, she said she could give me breakfast and supper, too, all for twelve dollars a week.

Maybe it was the twelve dollars that decided me, for a man making but twenty hardly had free choice. Maybe it was some quality in her, dimly sensed. Maybe it was the look in her magnified eyes. Anyhow, I moved in.

There wasn't much to move. The suit I wore, a shaggy garment far too heavy for Kentucky summer weather, was the only one I had. I owned a single pair of shoes, both worn through at the soles, which I repaired with cardboard day by day. A hat and a scattering of small clothes completed my wardrobe. My one other physical possession was a portable typewriter that I had clung to in the belief that someday I would write.

Maybe the landlady would let me type upstairs in leisure hours, though it was doubtful that she'd have much sympathy, not this old and surely humdrum though softspoken woman. What could be expected of her except a bed and meals? When bigger money came to me, I'd say goodbye and locate better quarters, owned and occupied by interesting and stimulating people.

Humdrum? Interesting? Stimulating?

On first encounter I didn't recognize a godsend.

In those times and for years to come, Lexington was a small and self-contained city, largely happy with the growth and marketing of burley tobacco, the breeding and racing of horses, the regional production of whiskey—and with tradition.

Perhaps most of all with tradition, for it was a caste-conscious town where the possessors of old names commanded a social esteem often out of proportion to all but their ancestry, which sometimes was shaky itself. No matter. Grandfather or Great-grandfather or old Uncle John was a noted soldier or a high political figure or the owner of a country estate once so famous that its name survived its dissolution. An unknown, unless he'd come to buy Thoroughbred yearlings, found the atmosphere chilly.

Later I was to reflect that a state rich in old history develops foolish distinctions out of attachment to history, and if the distinctions tend to filter down and be embraced class by class as part of the atmosphere, that can hardly be wondered at. The history was there, and the love of history, and these were important; and I came to wish that an interest in antecedents were as warm and alive in Montana, though when it is, I suppose, we'll have grown caste-conscious, too. Maybe we will in time, anyhow, for the aging state develops infirmities.

The Bluegrass landscape did not enchant me, though I was informed that it should. White paneled fences, manicured fields, gentle rolls of land, orderly trees—these smacked too much of man. They were artificial and ephemeral. I told myself, thinking of Montana, that I liked my beauty grim. I liked it out of control, pristine, everlasting as man's work could never be.

But comparisons of places, men and manners need the revision of experience. They become not so much comparisons as recognitions of differences, with neither the good nor the bad summoned to the support of prejudice. So it was that I came to feel as much at home in Kentucky as in Montana. They were in a sense opposing worlds, both known and both loved. And so it was that I could say later with a truth that still holds:

The satisfaction to be found in Kentucky isn't necessarily bushels to the acre, gain on the hoof or production on some industrial line. It can be laurel on a mountainside, the white shower of serviceberry, the wind ripple of bluegrass, the palisades of the Kentucky River, the spring festival of redbud and dogwood, the long haze of autumn, the columned front of old Morrison Chapel in Lexington. It can be a friend and a julep and a mare in a pasture. It can be the blaze of old cherry, fashioned after Hepplewhite. It can be a place where walk the ghosts of better men and worse. It can be a stage in the great American journey, east to west, where Dan'l Boone and George Rogers Clark and frontiersmen and soldiers and seekers tramped history on the land. It can be a day at the Lexington Trots or at Keeneland or Churchill Downs. It can be old ham and beaten biscuits and fried chicken and corn pudding.

These things the Kentuckian knows how to appreciate. Problems exist, troubles arise, but these endure.

The Kentuckian walks down the street of his town and meets friends along the way, and they stop, wanting to know how things are, how's the family, why'n't you come and see us, who you pickin' in the Derby, let's have a cup of coffee.

Or he and his wife call on their neighbors at night and, leaving, hear the words, "Glad you came. You all hurry back." Answering, they say, "You all come and see us now. Hear?" The partings are standard, but the sentiment is honest.

On other counts the Bluegrass was a good place to live in. In imagination, now that I am away, I hear with nostalgia the long songs of the katydids and the mockingbirds. In company with my friend, Cecil C. Carpenter, dean of Kentucky's department of commerce, I stop at a crossroads antique shop and dicker for an old rifle or a dilapidated chest of drawers that shows class beneath ruin, knowing something of values from Cecil's teachings. With Thomas D. Clark, later Kentucky's history department chairman, I spend rich evenings, talking of old times and new books, exchanging confessions of ambitions, for both of us are young and untried. I see the rich spring white and yellow and red and smell the good smells of blooms at first strange to my senses. Evening comes on, and the air is still and crickets sing from the grass, and the fed man sits on his step and asks himself what more he wants.

Lexington was leisurely, often even for a man with a deadline to meet. People in the heart of town, walking Main or Short or Limestone or Upper streets, seldom let business interfere with a chat. The place abounded in great and funny storytellers, among whom was William H. Townsend, attorney, writer and authority on Lincoln, whose recorded biographical speech about Cassius Marcellus Clay—not the loose-lipped boxer of the same name, for history's sweet sake!—ranks with the best of spoken narratives. (The recording can be purchased at just one place, the Morris Book Shop, Lexington.) Imaginative pranksters provided public glee. And characters! The town was full of them, most renowned but some obscure, whose acts and utterances, whether questionably attributed or true, went from tongue to tongue and made the air salubrious. And how superior these were to the manufactured jokes that conventioneers and traveling salesman found—and find—fun in repeating.

Before I came to such terms with Kentucky, I had

to accept and in a measure forgive the importance attached
to "acceptance."

Two or three weeks after I had reported for work in the
Leader's editorial room, I learned that my colleagues had
combined against me. They proposed to freeze me out, presumably, I gathered, because I was a foreigner without benefit of credentials, a man from nowhere, without claims to
acceptance. One of the conspirators, Joe Jordan, who became as good a friend as ever I had, denied these reasons
later. He said the plot developed because I looked impossibly
pious. The description was accurate, though I question the
assignment of motive.

Then one of the gang chanced on the fact that I came
from Montana. He had spent weeks in the West, as bellman
at Yellowstone Park and as assistant to his father, who arranged summer tours, and had visited Montana and liked the
place and its people. So Dan Bowmar renounced the con-
spiracy and became, like Joe Jordan, one of the handful of
devoted friends that any man is lucky to be able to count.

My co-workers weren't rude; they were just indifferent
and uncommunicative. I was too busy and excited to take
even due notice. At last I was a newspaperman, if only a cub,
not a country newspaperman, either, but a member of a staff
of a seven-day-a-week daily, whose subscribers numbered
nineteen or twenty thousand. I was what I was trained for, I
was what I wanted to be, and if my first assignments were
piddling, time and effort would lead me to big ones. Good
days. Happy days. Days of absorption and excitement.
Days of learning the community as only a newspaperman
learns a community. In hope, in growing assurance, in
young fulfillment, I was enchanted until the years wore the
shine off newspapermaking.

The names of that early staff, along with those of others who came along later, ring through the years—Dan Bowmar, Joe Jordan, Charlie Dickerson, Brownie Leach, Fred Jackson, Neville Dunn, Helen Howard, Lucille Myers.

If I looked pious, Dan looked saintly. Large-eyed, soft-spoken, courteous, methodical at work, he posed successfully as a preacher more than once, after having found revelation in the bottle. Sometimes he reversed his role, having had word from the devil, and spoke at riotous length on the machinery of the church or the Southern Railroad's responsibility for the growing population of the south side, where a train tooted its horn every morning at an hour too early for breakfast. He had his own theories on all subjects and his original antic moods, and we used to wait for alcohol to dissolve the lacquer of propriety.

A man had to watch out for Joe, whose humor was sharp and often barbed and sometimes calculated, whereas Dan's had no sting and seemed slowly spontaneous. A panhandler came to the newsroom one day, as panhandlers often did. It was his bad luck to encounter Joe first. The panhandler held out a card. It said its owner was deaf and dumb and in need of money. Dan was on the state desk, editing copy, his ministerial eyes downturned. Joe got up from his typewriter, pointed to Dan and pushed the man over. From behind the beggar Joe spoke. Dan's eyes flew up from his copy. His mouth fell open. Joe had said, "Dan, here's some dirty son of a bitch that wants to see you."

The man left. We never did know whether he was afflicted.

Both Dan and Joe were able and dedicated newspapermen. Both strove for an excellent paper. Each had his good way of work. Dan's was one of thoughtful method, Joe's one of fast yet accurate action. Both had had a year or two of experience, as I had not. Both knew the Kentucky I didn't. They were a challenge I'm grateful for.

One of the great Lexington characters was Dudley B. Veal, who after years as city detective won the race for county jailer. Though poorly schooled, he held vigorous opinions and had his own way of stating them. With matters in hand at the jail, he used to laze on Short Street, where we often saw him. It was his habit to scratch his back on any handy upright, a habit that led Ducky Drake, an attorney, to say that Dud "admired to strop his ass on a telephone pole."

We used to bait Dud, not in ridicule but in the hope of getting him going. "Dud," we asked him once, "how do you know the world is round?"

Dud considered, meantime stropping. Out of his long knowledge as an agent of the law, the answer came: "Because every no-good son of a bitch that ever left Lexington always came back."

What about perversion?

The reply was immediate. "It's a goddam dirty thing— I don't care how nice you go about it."

And what about a man who got up in the dark to go horseback riding?

"Who did?"

"Paul Revere."

Very funny, we thought in those days.

Dud shook his head. "Never heard tell of the son of a bitch."

I was covering the police beat one Saturday night. In charge as night chief was Captain Jim Donlon, a fine Irishman with a fine Irish accent.

In a straight chair tilted against a wall sat a newly elected justice of the peace, hoping to take in a few dollars as bondsman. An immense flatulence afflicted him, which he was at no pains to conceal. It would be unfair to say that the room resounded. It just kept being alerted.

There was no news that fitted printing, and I wandered off. When I came back, the man had left.

"He went out," Captain Donlon told me and added as a thought, without grinning, "You know, he far-rts more than inyone I ivver saw—on short acquaintance."

On another night, hot as a broken blister, I sweated slowly to the station. A sergeant sat outside with hardly the energy to fan himself. "All's quiet," he said with moist satisfaction. I took a chair close by.

Presently an angular and ill-favored colored woman climbed over the concrete wall that separated the Negro section of Chicago Bottoms from the station's parking lot. "Sahgent," she said, dripping perspiration, "I want a wahnt."

The sergeant wiped his face and asked her why.

"On account of a man," she told him. "In my house a man is breakin' in."

The sergeant was wise. "You been livin' with him, Auntie?"

"Not any more," she said. "Nevah no mo'."

The sergeant didn't move except to wipe his forehead again. "Why don't you just go home and give him a little lovin'?"

The colored woman drew herself up. "Sahgent, you know what stemmin' tobacco is? I stemmed fo'ty pounds today. Time you stem fo'ty pounds, you got no mind for lovin'—hot as it is."

There was a famous madam in the town, by name Belle
Breezing, whose house, decaying ever since the amateurs
took over, as they say, once had been known clear to the
Eastern seaboard, not only for its entertainment, but its ele-
gance. Girls, champagne, fine furniture, great gilded mir-
rors, gentility.

One day old Belle up and died.

At the auction of her effects—here I get a little ahead
of myself—the place was jammed with worthy women. The
Junior League, the American Association of University
Women, the D.A.R., the Woman's Club, the Altrusans and
others of the proper may have had a quorum each. The men,
themselves there in some numbers, put differing constructions on the incidence of females, but all grinned then and
afterwards, thinking either they were wiser or confirmed in
prior judgment.

Belle's death inspired one man of mark. He printed
letters edged in black, thanking men for their tokens of sympathy, and these he mailed to righteous families.

A young fellow went to work as reporter for what then
was our rival, the *Lexington Herald*. Wally, I'll call him.
Green as the most recent of journalism graduates, he was
assigned to the police department. One night—again it
was Saturday, just hours before the two papers, one morning and one afternoon, would compete simultaneously—
a truck ran into a tank filled with sewage pumped out
of cesspools and septic receptacles. Considerable spillage re-
sulted.

The notation on the police blotter said a truck had hit a
honey wagon.

Wally wrote the story. Honey all over one block of
Walnut Street. The deskman knew no better, either. He

wrote a headline and put the story on Page One. The head read: BEES WILL BE BUSY.

The timing was just fine for us, for then was the season of the year—March, I believe it was—when country peddlers walked the streets, importuning one and all to buy their pails of honey.

No, we'd say to them, we were well-stocked, but we knew a man not far away who'd been asking where to find some. We pointed to the opposition's building and gave them Wally's name. What happened when they showed up, I can't say, but Wally had caught on.

Still on the night police beat, Wally, it happened one evening then, was reading the peach edition of the *Louisville Times* in the station. The desk at which he was standing made a right-angle turn from which, as a ceiling support, rose a two-feet-square upright. It blocked Wally's sight from the phone just beyond it and from its users.

There entered a used-car salesman, a loud and explosive man who often came into the station just to see what was up. He went to the phone and rang home. "Hello, Honey," he said to his wife.

Wally dropped the *Times*, charged around the upright and kicked his best kick in the stooped-over pants. The telephone fell with a clatter. The salesman was punching before he got in position. Wally was already swinging. Three cops, it took, to separate them—and neither knew the other.

With such bits of comedy we regaled ourselves in those young days. Life was good and joyous, and, if it tended to lag, we found things to spur it.

Even in those first days, when Lexington was chilly, there was always Mary Lizzie.

I'd take the bus and from the nearest stop walk the blocks to her house, feeling low in mind. Not only was I unwelcome in town, but the girl I had wanted so long to marry on nothing had gotten engaged to a miller, to a son and grandson of millers of wealth. A notice had appeared in the *Choteau Acantha.*

But maybe the postman had delivered the *American Mercury* or the *Nation,* and I could read for an hour or two before being called to supper.

So one or the other of the journals had arrived, and, after calling hello to Mary Lizzie, I'd hunch down in a chair and open it.

Then from the kitchen, where Mary Lizzie forever was preparing something special for me, she'd call in that voice that is in my ears yet, "Buddy. Oh, Buddy."

And I knew out of experience that she was about to breach a bottle of home-made wine.

There came to Lexington that summer or that fall the Meeting of the running horses, the Thoroughbreds, who or which—depending on your upbringing—would put their speeds to test. They would race at the Kentucky Association track, which later was relinquished and, by public housing, devoted to the race of human procreation. It was a chummy place, the Kentucky Association, far better than the present Keeneland.

One afternoon of racing I had seen, and that at old Latonia, just outside Cincinnati. I won a little money, too, betting on a mare named Ethel Waters. That was just before I went to work in Lexington. Pending my employment date, I was the guest in Cincinnati of an aunt and uncle. My aunt was a lady with that touch of outrage without which I deem people dull. Of all my lateral relatives she was my favorite. Mark her name: It was Clyde Witt, and, again, she was a lady.

Weekdays I worked from half past seven until four. Saturdays I had to show up, again at half past seven, and work sometimes into the morning, into dawn, for our Sunday sheet disliked being put to bed. With luck a man might have a few hours off when once the half-day Saturday edition had been fed into the presses. I was in luck. Next Saturday I could enjoy a lapse.

I wrote my aunt, Clyde Witt, and asked her down. Together we'd attend the races. Her answer was prompt. She'd come, and in good time. Cincinnati was less than three hours distant even by a careful car.

Money was my problem. I had passes to the races and change enough for bus fare but hardly more than that.

I took my typewriter down to Rosenberg's. The man said fifteen dollars. I told him sixteen, not a penny less. You couldn't bet a single dollar on a race, not that fifteenth that might remain to me. He counted out sixteen.

Saturday morning Aunt Clyde wired. She couldn't meet me after all. Something had come up.

With all arrangements made and money in my pocket, I chose, though disappointed, to go then by myself.

I arrived a little early, fifteen or twenty minutes before post time for the first race. I bought a program and started leafing through it. The fifth race was for maiden two-year-old fillies. A maiden is a runner that has never won a race, whether in competition or for lack of opportunity. In this case most of the entries were first-starters, and from among them a name leaped out. The name was Lady Witt.

Four races went by without a bet from me. I stood at

the rail, clutching my program, opened at the fifth. My thumbnail put a dent in Lady Witt.

Without thought of odds, without consideration of the handicapper's picks, I went to the win window then and put all my sixteen dollars on the Lady. No across-the-board bet. No place or show. Every nickel on the nose.

In the paddock, as they saddled her, she didn't look like much. Small, for one thing, especially to eyes accustomed to ranch animals. Thin, too. She hardly drew a glance from the wiser men who crowded me. I fingered the bus fare that would get me back to town.

The bugle sounded. The outrider started from the paddock, leading a dancing filly. The other entries followed. Lady Witt still looked outclassed.

She was fractious at the post, the most fractious of the bunch. Finally an assistant starter put a twitch on her and forced her to the line.

"Go!" came the call, and Lady Witt went. Within a few strides she opened up a good lead and kept increasing it. But you never know. Runners with early foot often fade away. Not so Lady Witt. She was never headed. She crossed the line a winner by at least a stone's throw.

By and by her price was posted. Forty-four twenty! Forty-four twenty for two! Eight times forty-four twenty?

I won the next two races, too, without going for broke, and wound up a winner by some six or seven hundred dollars. I hastened home, where I'd have time to tell Mary Lizzie of my luck before reporting back for duty.

Mary Lizzie gloated at the stack of bills. Peremptorily she took it, saying, "I'll keep it for you, so you don't feel niggah rich."

I told her I had to have $350 of it. She asked why, and

I explained. Reluctantly she counted out the sum. It was enough to pay back Mr. Sands and the Bank of Attica and get my typewriter out of hock besides.

But now she continued, "Next week, after work, you go see my old friend Mike Rogers, and buy yourse'f some clothes and shoes. He'll trust you, knowing me." She waved the money that she had in her hand. "I'll give you moah when we find out what the bill is."

She got up. "And now it's time for celebratin', as we used to say in Bardstown." She went down into the cellar and came back with a jug of home-made wine. "Can't let good luck go by," she went on, "and what if you're a minute late?" She looked at the jug. "Our wine is goin' fast." With that she poured two tumblers full.

Seated, with the welcome glass in her old hand, she told me, "Buddy, I reckoned you would win. Yistiddy I went down to St. Peter's and lit a candle for you."

She added, as if the description had just occurred to her, "Here's to you, Buddy—the blue hen's chick."

7

Our managing editor in those early years consisted of a pipe, a bluster and a faint heart. He used the whip to cover his shakiness, and it took a little time or a friendly tip to find you could disarm him. Faced up to, he socketed the whip, and first thing you knew, he had his hand on your shoulder, his pipe out of his teeth and his mouth full of compliments.

He lived in terror of libel suits and consequently mutilated our copy. John Doe, if he was in trouble with the law, wasn't John Doe; he was a man "reputed to be John Doe" or "said by police to be John Doe" or "booked as John Doe." Our man, we used to say, would be uncertain of his own identity if he found himself in jail. A bare recital of facts, if it reflected on anyone, had to be conditioned. His favorite conditioner, set between commas and inserted more or less at random in suspect sentences, was "so the story goes."

I shouldn't complain. His caution got me my job. O.K. Barnes, a young man whom I met later, had written a gag, using repeatedly all the m.e.'s safety devices plus a few artful dodges of his own. By accident his takeoff got into the copy basket and went to the printers, who gleefully put it in type. Again quite by accident the proof fell under the gaze of the boss. So came the end of O.K. on the *Leader* and the beginning of me.

The m.e. hardly knew good copy from bad. If ever he had heard of parallelisms or the sequence of tenses, he held the knowledge too precious for practice, as do too many newsmen, if they've heard, to this day.

He took pride in his headlines, and no wonder. In the neighboring town of Richmond a hospital patient died soon after eating his lunch. While it was and is a miracle to me that more patients don't succumb to hospital fare, it remained for the m.e. to add two and two. He captioned the obit:

EATS DILL PICKLE, DIES

A contributor, or stringer, to a number of big-city dailies, which accepted his copy with amazing credulity, he slavered over what he called human-interest stories. A small country girl rode a turkey to school. Or so the story goes. Another fell ill when told there was no Santa Claus. Ah, but there was. Gifts from all over began to pile up at the small railroad station near which, by report, she languished. No subsequent story of his reported that no one could find her.

In the oil fields east of Lexington a crew made a pet of a big country dog. The well being drilled showed some promise, and it was decided to shoot it. Came a morning so nippy

that the explosive required warming up before use. It was
poured into a basin and set near the fire. While the men
waited, inattentively, the dog licked it up. Then discovery.
Then panic. Away the men sprinted, in all directions, and
after them, from one to another, bounded the living bomb,
happy with the game. A flushed rabbit averted calamity.
The dog took off after it. The rabbit ducked under a fence.
The dog tried to jump it, caught his foot and fell and went
boom. Nothing remained of him, not even a hair, but a great
hole in the ground marked where he'd hit.

The story has an unreported but hardly more credible
sequel. A New York paper grew dubious and sent a reporter
to determine the facts. The *Leader's* stringer, who had submitted the facts in the first place, was fazed not at all. He
took the visitor to an abandoned rock quarry and said,
"There's the hole."

Yet we couldn't really dislike James M. Ross. We knew
he did his poor best in a too-busy position, and we saw him
more as a man miscast than as an incompetent and often
unpleasant boss. And we agreed on one virtue of his. He
knew Kentucky names and backgrounds and, thus qualified,
often saw stories where less informed editors didn't.

Charlie Dickerson, the city editor, was a first-rate newspaperman, but was too gentle and self-contained for command. One time Joe Jordan, then on the police beat, called
the newsroom just before deadline. Charlie answered. Joe
said he had a hot story. Charlie said he'd take it. Joe dictated:

"According to Chief of Police Ernest Thompson, Assistant Chief Austin B. Price, Night Chief James Donlon, as
well as Police Court Clerk Dudley McCloy and . . ."

Then Joe started reading the whole roster.

Charlie industriously put down a half a dozen or more

names before he caught on. I like to remember that he began laughing then.

Under those early circumstances, if we were to learn at all, we had to learn by ourselves. We did so by banterings, sly digs and sober discussions. We educated ourselves—and in more than craftsmanship. After I had become city editor, Joe said to me once, "It's all right to direct, but you don't have to act like a top sergeant." That piece of advice stays me to this day.

The owner of the *Leader* was a friendly and unpretentious man who knew nothing of newspapermaking but did know that the future of the Republic resided in the Republican party. Most of the editorials were written by an aging Presbyterian minister who addressed himself with mild earnestness to country congregations on Sundays. His loves were Prohibition, the Bible, and the bootstrap five-year-plan strivings of the Russians, whom he considered the unhappy but amiable and indomitable creatures of circumstance.

Yet with the encouragement of a then young general manager and out of our own sense of the responsibility that freedom imposes on the press, we got out a good and unshrinking paper, one almost never suppressed in its coverage, if only because most of us wouldn't work under trespass.

It fell largely to me, as the newest-comer to the staff, to do what nobody else wished to. The managing editor was always running out of tobacco. I fetched it for him. Or he wanted an apple. Or he needed time copy and kept me after hours getting it out. Time copy, if an explanation is needed, is copy with little or no timely importance and serves to fill holes in pages, for to leave a blank is unholy.

It was our custom, during the fund drive for the Community Chest, to print year-end roundups about member agencies. Among others, I drew the Florence Crittenton

Home, which the paper had avoided before, not wanting, I suppose, to put in at so touchy a port.

The matron was ready for me. At least she had the girls tucked out of sight and the babies all on display. But this was her first newspaper interview, and her breath came fast as she showed me from crib to crib and applauded each tiny tenant. With shaky pride she told me how the place had grown since first established, how many girls had sought and been granted refuge in the last year.

She followed me to the door and, as I opened it, exclaimed, "Oh, Mr. Guthrie. I'm so encouraged. Every year, it seems to me, our girls are of a higher and higher class."

I didn't know what to make of that.

Promotions in function and title came to me quickly, through resignations and dismissals and want of active competition as much as through merit. By 1927 I was writing editorials in support of the Republican party and its choice for governor. I covered the ensuing session of the legislature and, through the years, a score or so more, regular and special, and learned early the importance of liquor to legislation. I was made city editor, managing editor and finally executive editor.

But titles don't mean much in newspapermaking. The man elevated in rank is likely to find himself doing the same old things almost for the same old money. Nominal promotion and financial reward don't always go hand in hand. And more often than not editorial salaries are so low as to make ridiculous the cries of publishers over the absence of bright young candidates for the newsroom and the departures of seasoned reporters for positions in public relations, radio and TV. While managing a staff and doing more incidental chores than I like to think about, I used to write editorials, for I got a dollar extra for each one published and was happy to get it.

My desk faced the entry, and physical as well as official position made me the main greeter of visitors—complainers, seekers of space, sources with sure-enough news, and friends who couldn't understand why I gave them short shrift. The owner couldn't understand, either. He often came in, usually with a story to tell. Under the pressure of deadlines I sometimes excused myself and hurt his uncomprehending feelings. He asked the general manager why I didn't like him.

For the Negro population—and the Republican party —we ran what we called Colored Notes. They reported and repeated, day after day, religious and social doings. A favorite festivity was the Heaven and Hell party. The losers ate chili, the winners ice cream. The notes, mostly handwritten on scraps of paper, settled on my desk like ragged drifts of leaves, and for years I had to find the frenzied time to edit them. Some of the little fun in that chore disappeared when a girls' club named the Ten Virgins petered out.

Headlining was harder then than in these days of easy and ragged non-style. We believed in balance—which is to say that headlines had to be flush with the column rules left and right or uniformly indented from the first line on down, with no more difference in length between or among them than the room occupied by an em or at most an em and a half. That wasn't all. Good headlines, we said, had to be enclytic, never proclytic. We meant—if the terms are not clear—that the first line had to hold a meaning in itself, enlarged or modified by the second line, which in turn didn't hang on the third.

We took pride in the results, perhaps with some justice. I'm inclined to think so when I see what passes for headlines these days. The one merit of the ragged style is that it's fast.

Any deskman who can read can slap something on top of a news story without thinking twice. The achievement of balance took time, though practice shortened it. I got so I thought in column widths. Example:

MOON   ORBITING
FAR   FROM   NEW,
COW   MAINTAINS

Nowadays the same story might be headlined:

COW SAYS SHE
WENT OVER
MOON FIRST

I had to watch my associates. They'd slip to the composing room, as Colored Notes, Sunday sermon themes at non-existent houses of worship. There come to mind: "The Goneness of the Past," "To See Saint Peter, Put Your Headlights On" and "The Inevitable Shall Not Come to Pass." Sly practice aside from Colored Notes needed but sometimes didn't get the editorial eye. Once, having to leave the desk, I asked Dan Bowmar to take over. A story from city hall came to him instructing householders how best to put out for collection their coal-furnace ashes. Dan marked it Page One and over it posted this headline:

CITY   INSPECTOR   EXPLAINS
HOW TO GET ASHES HAULED

I braced myself after the paper came out but received not a single complaint. So our readers, by conclusion, must have belonged in three classes: (1) those who were ignorant, (2) those who weren't but were tickled, (3) those who knew but were too upright to acknowledge exposure to the back-alley idiom.

I remember those days as the heydays of impostors, pretenders and bums, and of kids and crazy adults crazy for lines in the paper. Tree sitters nested in trees; a man was rolling a hoop from East Coast to West and stopped by to relate the glad news; riding the grub line from one patriots' post to another, professional veterans of the First World War annually came to the newsroom bearing clippings they wanted to add to; a man with that hard dedication that frightens the lost shook loose from the litter in a two-quart jar a brood of blond mice. Diet, he said, had blanched their coats. In a race-torn society, think! We fell for a boy who posed as the prizefighter, Sammy Mandell. He couldn't have pushed home a thumb tack. We supported with full heart a sculptor, who had learned his craft, it later transpired, in a penitentiary, not in the studios abroad that he mentioned. Evangelists in sermon and song kept saving us. One had to his credit "The Old Rugged Cross," which is younger than young and old think. He wouldn't let a photographer take his picture. He insisted on one taken long, long ago. Only the cross had grown old.

And panhandlers! It used to be said, and maybe still is, that, next to a parsonage, a newsroom was the easiest touch. I was touched time and again and, because trust expands life, dislike to report that never a penny came back.

8

I have been one-sided about Mary Lizzie and must say here and now, before telling more stories about her, that she was a lady of quality, a too-generous spirit, a woman of outrage assuredly but one of high morals also and of a quick and deep and diverting mind. If she liked to drink, it was never to numb her felt obligations. When she used improper expressions, as she often did, the words came in revolt against pretense and primness and over-pitched piety.

Suspicious of priests outside the realm of the spirit, she had been and kept being a good Catholic. As long as she was able she trudged the long blocks to mass and confession; and many a time, when it appeared I might get a break, she walked the long blocks again and for my luck lighted a candle. More than once we rejoiced and gave thanks to St. Anthony.

She abhorred illicit sex. When she heard that a small house she owned and rented to Negroes was being used as a brothel, she ejected the tenants, though all the saints must have known she needed the money.

She spent more on my meals than I ever paid. Afoot she went to the markets and bought what I liked, no matter the cost. Breakfast and supper were ample beyond appetite, but, she said, a boy making only twenty dollars a week and having but one pair of shoes and one suit couldn't afford money for lunch and so had to have two oversize meals. She washed my clothes, too—on a board in a dirt-floored basement that sometimes was knee-deep in water.

I didn't mind, indeed rather relished, her secret readings of my letters from home. She betrayed herself by insisting that I came from a mighty fine family and so must make the most of myself.

Mary Lizzie had received—partly as a result of her native intelligence—a good education in a convent, where she learned but did not altogether endorse the rigidities of the true faith. Once she had been a promising pianist and still retained much knowledge of music. She knew about the usage of English as well, and soon could spot, nine times out of ten, the special stories I'd written.

After I'd come to her house, other young men, never more than two at a time, rented rooms and took board, and a couple complained at the special treatment I got. They said she called me, who had to be first out of bed, in the gentlest of tones, whereas she screamed up the stairway to awaken them later on.

Without apology she told them in so many words that I

was the blue hen's chick. And so I was, and was well content to be.

I spent five years at her house and wed my wife there, wed the girl, that is, who'd thrown me over but who dropped by for a visit on a trip from the East, intending in a day or two to take the train for Montana. But for Mary Lizzie she might not have married me then. "Harriet Larson," Mary Lizzie kept telling her while I was at work, "if I had a daughter, you'd never have the chance to marry Bud Guthrie."

Harriet liked her and came, too, to love her, as I knew she would. Once a week, nearly always, after we'd found our own quarters, we went to see her; and always on feast days she was our guest.

It is truth to say that no one, hardly excluding our parents, so shaped our lives and no one at all gave us more joy.

Mary Lizzie had a rich, shirt-tail relative who liked to bet on the races. Next Saturday, he wrote once, he would come to Lexington for an afternoon at the track—and could Mary Lizzie, despite Prohibition, find him a case of good whiskey?

The assignment was risky in those days, but through old connections Mary Lizzie got the case smuggled into the house. It was very fine whiskey, called, incredibly, Old Chicken Cock, and it cost twenty dollars a bottle.

Clarence, as I shall call him, showed up at the house about noon, along with a friend. They had a few drinks and took off for the track, leaving with Mary Lizzie eleven quart bottles that they'd pick up later. I got home before they were back.

"Bud," Mary Lizzie announced as I opened the door,

"come have a drink of red whiskey. Clarence didn't have the manners to offer me one, after all the trouble and danger I went to, so I stole a bottle out of the case there."

"They'll notice it, Mary Lizzie," I said. "How you going to explain it?"

"It'll surely come to me," she answered. "After a drink or two it'll come to me."

We had a couple apiece before Clarence and his friend came back from the track. The ponies hadn't run true to form, and both wished to console themselves with Old Chicken Cock. Mary Lizzie served them while they beefed about their hard luck. Meantime she and I took a nip in the kitchen.

Time to start home, they said finally. Time to pick up the case and disguise it and stash it in the trunk of their car.

Clarence got up and went to the carton. "One's missing," he said. He hadn't accumulated his cash by being careless.

Mary Lizzie met him eye to eye. "Must be you took two to the track, I reckon."

Clarence answered, "No!"

"I paid for twelve bottles," she told him, "and you paid me back. Now, Clarence, you and your friend had some drinks here before post time. I was a right smart worried about you, drivin' and all. It must be you took a bottle apiece."

Clarence swore they hadn't.

"I declare," Mary Lizzie said. "Did you count them when you opened the case?"

Clarence had to admit that he hadn't.

Mary Lizzie shook her head. "That shows you. Somebody lifted a bottle while on the way here. These days, you can't trust anyone."

Clarence got up, summoned his friend, said a bobtailed goodbye, picked up what was left of the case and departed.

"Bud," Mary Lizzie said after the door had been slammed, "I must go to confession, I reckon. To steal is to sin. Let's have another drink while I think."

I followed her toward the kitchen. At the door she came to a halt and turned to face me. She spoke in that soft voice, without "r's," that can't be represented on paper. "But you reckon the Lord loves a short sport?"

Mary Lizzie had a fine sense of contrast, and I repeat here a story, with authorial intrusions, that I sometimes could get her to tell.

Fresh out of high school, she qualified as a schoolteacher by answering a single question correctly. What was a coot? "I come from haunts of coot and hern," she quoted from Tennyson and went on to explain that both were waterfowl.

The examiner was an old friend of the family and passed her forthwith; but I have a picture of her taken in that year and think her comeliness was as great a factor as friendship.

She got a position right away, at a country crossroads where a distillery was located. It was arranged, before she took off by stagecoach, that she stay at the home of the owner.

Either she arrived a day earlier than expected or the mistress of the house, having been negligent, said that she had. Married women in parts of Kentucky are often called Miss, and I'll call this one Miss Minnie, thus combining custom and caution, for Minnie wasn't her name. She was not only not ready to lodge Mary Lizzie; she was a long way from sober.

"Law me, child!" she said. "It was tomorrow we reckoned on, me and the Mister. But he's out of town for the night, and you can come sleep with me. First thing in the morning, we'll get your room tidied up."

The house was an old one with a gallery or breezeway upstairs that led back to quarters for servants. There wasn't but one man on the place now, Miss Minnie said, and you couldn't call him a man, him being but eighteen or less.

All during the evening and later, when the two were in bed, Miss Minnie kept taking leave of her roomer and coming back freshened in breath.

"Miss Minnie," Mary Lizzie said finally through the effluvium, "is there a little drink in the house? I'm kind of crampin'."

"Law no, honey," Miss Minnie answered. "Not as much as a drop. But tomorrow when the Mister comes home, he'll get us some from the still."

On the last of her returns from the bottle Miss Minnie fell flat on the floor and cracked her skull on what Mary Lizzie in proper moments identified as the night urn.

Between booze and bump Miss Minnie had had it, nor could Mary Lizzie alone lift or arouse her. There was, though, the hired hand yon side of the gallery. Mary Lizzie ran and routed him out and chased on his heels to the casualty. He took Miss Minnie's shoulders, Mary Lizzie her legs, and together they managed to hoist her and put her, stomach up, in her bed.

It was then that she opened her eyes and stared at the boy. "Are you," she asked, "Jesus Chirst?"

"No, Miss Minnie!" he said. "I'm not Jesus Christ. I'm Lee Pendergast."

That first fall and winter at her house Mary Lizzie and I drank the place dry. Spring came, and drouth, and we had no funds for outside relief. Even moonshine cost two or three dollars a pint. Then a May morning dawned, pregnant with promise.

"Bud," Mary Lizzie said while I was at breakfast, "this evenin' come straight home from work. The dandelions will be in full bloom. You can pick them. I'll put them to set with a dose of yeast and cornmeal like my distiller friend told me, and shortly we'll have somethin' to drink."

That afternoon was warm and slow with the onset of spring fever. On our street, as I hastened home, men back from work sat on front porches, pleasantly sweating, and housewives sat with them, reluctant to cook while the sun smiled away winter. Vegetating, they watched me, and a sense of guilt overtook me that young people these days won't understand. In many minds alcohol equated with sin, and even the wets, as they called them, felt the brush of the wing of public damnation.

To hold my pickings Mary Lizzie had hauled out and placed in the backyard a light plywood box big enough to contain a piano. I plucked the blooms and pitched them in. But when I started to horse that great box around to the front, I saw the neighbors looking, no doubt for evil and food for talk, and I let go the box and mounted the side-entry stairs.

"Mary Lizzie," I said, "I can't do it. Everyone's watching."

She bustled down the steps, saying, "You're a damn moral coward."

I trailed her to the front lawn, and there, watched by all the porch vegetables, she took to all fours and began picking and throwing, looking through and over her glasses as distance demanded.

I was too craven to help. I stood on one foot, then the other, thinking Prohibitionist thoughts while my lidded eyes traveled the street.

Now, up from Maple Avenue, appeared the Methodist minister, bound for the parsonage just a few doors beyond us. He was a little man with a little mustache and large dedication.

I kept still, Mary Lizzie kept plucking and chucking, and the preacher kept coming. Abreast of her, he halted and said, "Good afternoon, Mrs. Keating."

The greeting arrested her. She looked over her glasses, and guilt was inside her. "Oh, Reverend, thank you. Good evenin'."

He asked what she was doing.

It seemed a long time before Mary Lizzie replied. He couldn't see her gears grinding. "Well," she said, drawing the word out while the gears ground, "you see, the dandelions have taken my yahd, and a friend of mine told me if I burned the blooms then I'd be shed of them." She finished with some satisfaction.

"Oh, no, Mrs. Keating," he told her and reached in his pocket and got out a jackknife and sprang the big blade. "Let me show you."

He took hold of a plant and cut it off deep at the roots and went to another, then another, and more. The kindly deed done, he straightened and wiped off the blade and folded it home and reached for his pants pocket. "That's the way, Mrs. Keating," he said. "You've just been wasting your time."

Her voice was meek. "Reverend, thank you."

Still on hands and knees, Mary Lizzie watched him mince up the street.

Then she turned, glaring over her glasses, and said, "Bud, that son of a bitch has ruined our crop."

One of our neighbors was a retired registered nurse, a spinster who had gone through years of bedpans and enemas without losing a painful propriety. She was lonely, as was Mary Lizzie, and often came over to chat.

I found them in the kitchen one morning when I went in for breakfast. Both were outraged by the boys residing near by and their reckless discharges of air rifles.

"You know, Bud," Mary Lizzie said while she dished up my eggs, "Bernice was hit once."

"That so, Miss Bernice?" I asked in prebreakfast stupor. "Where was it?"

Miss Bernice sucked in a long breath.

Mary Lizzie waited as long as she could, then announced, "In the ass."

Miss Bernice left us.

Mary Lizzie liked, or submitted to, the ceremony of mass, but preachments annoyed her. After any priest preached a sermon, she'd come home rebellious. Who was he to be lecturing people? More than once after mass, while she was getting my breakfast, I'd ask, to bait her, "How was the service?" If the priest had gone past what she considered his sphere, she'd answer, "The damn fool!"

It came about that a Dutch priest came to the parish. He had a stern sense of mission and, unlike most Irish priests, no sense of humor. But the parish determined to get him a car, and undertook, by one means or another, to raise the money for it. For maximum service a priest needed wheels.

I was at home when the telephone rang and Mary Lizzie picked up the receiver. Half the conversation I heard, the other half she reported.

It was Mrs. O'Day, or someone of true Irish name, who was calling.

"Mrs. Keating," she said, "to help buy the Father a car, as chairman for the Sodality, I'm raffling off a canary. Will you buy a ticket? It's just fifty cents."

Every word, up to the danglers, Mary Lizzie uttered in answer with her soft-spoken gentility.

What she said was, "Well, Mrs. O'Day, if there's one thing I don't want, it's a cana'y bird—shitten all over my house."

Years later, at Harvard on a Nieman Fellowship, I met Theodore Morrison of the English department. I told him my stories about Mary Lizzie. He was delighted. He said I must get her on paper.

Get her on paper!

Who would believe? How make her live? In fiction of one kind or another? My Most Unforgettable Character? It is not until now, in this scattered approach to the people I've known, that I have even tried to approach her.

Some time after *The Big Sky* found print, Ted came to Lexington to speak at the University of Kentucky, where I was teaching, and I took him to see Mary Lizzie.

She was really old now and sometimes undone by the years and the loss of kinsfolk and friends and the knowledge that what remained of her life wasn't long; but she was in fine form that afternoon. She told about the Bardstown of her youth, about old friends and acquaintances and incidents. She told about Lee Pendergast, who was not Jesus Christ. She told about Mrs. White, the Bardstown wash-woman, who boasted that the youngest of her four daughters was doing the best of them all, harlottin' in Chicago. Whatever the subject, she had the illustration and the rare turn of speech.

I didn't listen too closely, knowing her stories and manner. It was better to watch Ted and see his great relish and to watch her and think how much I owed her. I had sat and absorbed her, in a sense, often over a drink, oftener over nary a drop, and learned more of Kentucky than many a native was ever to know; and the knowledge I got had assisted me, beyond easy reckoning, in my life as a Bloody Ground newspaperman and beyond any reckoning in my total career. The accidents of acquaintance are as important as purpose or what some call "gifts" in the course of a man. Courage and independence and stout attitudes, these had grown in me because I'd known her. From Ted had come to me the same sort of enforcement plus an over-all generosity in giving of the great deal that he knew about writing. So, thus indebted, it was better I sat, keeping silent, and observed and enjoyed the exchange.

Mary Lizzie was eighty or thereabouts then and, as she said, quoting others, had sailed the blue seas. She was a young woman, and pregnant, when the fancy harness horse her husband had bought her reared and fell back at the scream of a whistle. She had miscarried of injuries and been made forever infertile. Her husband, an engineer, had died later, while she was still young, and she had devoted nine years of her days to his father, who was gentle, she said, and a good man.

She was left with her old house, a couple of cheap rental properties and two or three thousand dollars in waterworks bonds and had had to take in roomers and boarders.

I'm not reporting her conversation with Ted. She never complained, but this much I already knew.

It came time to go.

At the door Mary Lizzie's old face started to collapse, but she took a breath and drew herself up with old courage.

"Young man," she told Ted, "next time you see me I'll probably be a-straddle of the throne of grace—or more likely in hell where all my friends are."

Mary Lizzie? Mary Lizzie. If there is any justice in the universe or any truth in your religion, you are riding high.

9

The best-known personage in the Bluegrass was not—
and to date is not—a statesman or a politician or an owner
of a horse farm or a collector and singer of ancient ballads
like John Jacob Niles or an historian and author like my old
friend and neighbor, Dr. Thomas D. Clark, who broke from
the wicker of Mississippi's cotton and cane and struck an
unbusheled light. It wasn't even Happy Chandler, who set
out to win national prominence with no more than a red
sweater and a five-dollar bill. It was a colored man, a hospital
orderly, James Herndon by name, whom most people knew
as Sweet Evening Breeze.

Hospital folk, those in position to measure his talents,
rated James the best of all orderlies. No one else could ad-

minister so artful an enema. When learners bungled the job, he was quick to inform and correct them. With the contents of the bag transmitted to the receiver, he slowed the imperative peristalsis with philosophical musings. All other tasks that fell to an orderly he performed with like competence.

His small house, which he himself kept, was immaculate, said those who knew, and furnished tastefully with antiques. He was known as an excellent cook, of pastries particularly.

But not even the sum of these virtues accounted for his fame.

James was effeminate in movement, response and, to a degree, dress. His voice was light, his walk short-stepped and mannered. He liked to groom himself and in public to appear in clean, pressed hospital whites. Once he was the featured performer, as reported in Colored Notes, in a Negro extravaganza. Lowered in a basket from the ceiling of Woodland Auditorium, decked out in feminine frills, he danced the Passion Dance of the Bongo Bangoes. I regret that I didn't see it.

No one questioned the inspired appropriateness of his nickname, though no one knew its origin, but everyone knew Sweet Evening Breeze, including outsiders with only a casual acquaintance with Lexington.

It came to pass, by the sworn word of witnesses, that in the days of Dud Veal as city detective James was brought to the station house for an offense imagined or real. One of Dud's fellow sleuths was Joe Harrigan, who was a shade the more literate.

Dud took the arrest blotter and laboriously began making the entry. Then he looked up at Harrigan. "I don't know what to book him for," he said.

Harrigan chewed on a cigar and sized up James. "Book him," he said, "for bein' a goddam proverb."

Two legal records, one phony, amused men of robust humor in Lexington.

The false one, dated 1882 and much copied, purported to be the indictment of a Metcalfe County man for publicly exposing himself; and the remarkable thing, its broad humor aside, was that it was accepted as true even by lawyers, though anyone could have arrived at the facts by a visit to the courthouse at Edmonton, distant from Lexington by only a couple of hours.

The text said that one William Yates betook himself to a church house and, in the presence of worshipers, while a minister of the gospel was holding forth, did there and then "unlawfully, willfully and maliciously extract, draw out of and pull from his trousers, breeches or pantaloons..." Guess what? The grand jury, deaf to the delicacy I exercise here, identified it by a goodly number of names, correct and indecorous, presumably to preclude any thought that he might have extracted anything else. With wavings and shakings, gesticulations and "divers sundry flirtations," the charge said, he let go "in vast quantities of a quart, pint or other measure, upon a red-hot stove, then and there standing, causing the same to fume, fizzle and give forth various, sundry and divers noxious odors, much to the disgust of the good people then and there assembled," and, what's more, he did "say, utter and speak from his lips the following, indecent, scurrilous language: 'By God, all who cannot swim will now mount the high bench, for the Great He Elephant is about to make water . . .' "

Next case.

Fledgling attorneys in Kentucky were introduced quickly to the case of Hardin *v.* Harshfield, which the curious may find in Volume 12 of the Kentucky Decisions of the

Court of Appeals. One attorney told me, indeed, that he had been made acquainted with it at Yale, so it is hard to say how far and into what citadels this piece of jurisprudence has penetrated.

The facts of the case are rather simple. A Bullitt County girl sued a slanderer, whose false and scatological story about her had induced her suitor to break off their engagement. A lower court ruled against her, and she appealed. That was eighty years and more ago.

The solemn justices gave solemn thought, or so their reversal of the first verdict indicates. Words didn't have to be actionable in themselves, they set out. It was enough that words, harmless per se, be intoned in a manner and accompanied by gestures such as to make them injurious by imputation. Neither did the words have to be heard in the first place by the person affected, in this instance by the fiancé. So long as he was affected to the injury of anyone, specifically the girl, then it didn't matter whether he heard the slander as originally uttered or as reported by others. In either case the orginator was accountable.

By the nature of the suit and the times and probably its own constitution the court couldn't conclude its opinion without some brave blows for the delicate and the doughty. After setting forth that slander could injure any manner of men, the good jurists went on:

"The reason is much stronger for protecting defenseless and helpless woman against false and malicious imputations, that tend to humiliate and degrade them in society. Kentucky manhood demands that they should be protected, and the guilty party mulcted in damages commensurate with the humiliation and degradation thus inflicted."

What was the slander? Here, quoted from the decision, are the words of the slanderer:

"Cordie Hardin [the girl] went to the store of Chris

Pauley to buy some groceries, and while Chris Pauley was waiting on her she let a big fart that was heard all over the room. Two or three young men being present, Chris Pauley looked at them and laughed, and they walked out of doors. Chris Pauley having fixed up the groceries, she took them, left the house and got on her horse, and forgot her gloves. She got down, and came back in the store. He supposed she was demoralized by what she had done, the fact being impressed on her mind so strongly. She said when she came back into the store, 'Mr. Pauley, did you see anything of that fart I let in here a while ago?' His reply was, 'No, but I smelt it damn strong.' Boys, ain't that a damned hard one on her?"

Laughable first, but much besides—the Big Fart Case, as it is known.

A Kentucky statute would protect the weak from corruption and may be employed against what I've just written. It puts within police-court jurisdiction the sale of "obscene" publications.

While the bill was being debated, a Senate supporter said to the applause of Kentucky motherhood that anyone knew what was obscene. Yes. Sure. It is as plain as the nose on your face. Hence it is the right, nay, the duty, of him who is pure in heart, let him be man of letters or labor, parishioner or preacher, to warn the bookseller of sin on his shelves. If the seller sells his filth nonetheless, he does so "knowingly" and thus breaks the law. Fine him! Throw him in jail! Or both!

A small matter, this local blister, and one not worth reporting except that it has far-and-wide company in the spotted fever of censorship and invites a disclosure of my personal practice and belief.

In writing, I do not use so-called bad words for shockers. I use them when they seem right, and only then. I am aware of the difference in impact between words heard and read, spoken and printed. Bernard DeVoto, speaking to this point, said that one "goddam" on a page was worth twelve, and twelve on a page were worth nothing. Out of boredom, out of the feeling that the writer lacks craftsmanship, I dislike prose that for any reason abounds in four-letter words. It follows that James Jones and Norman Mailer and Henry Miller are not for me, though I oppose any ban on their works. And I wonder, assuming for the moment that words are the soul-shapers that censors assert, which harms people more, the honest illumination or the doll-house reconstruction of life. Are youngsters prepared for encounter and challenge, for adversity, evil and full ecstasy, who have read only the perfumed and truncated versions of human experience that their elders call wholesome? A young man on perpetual make told me once that churches provided the best hunting grounds.

I've been tempted at times in censored communities to attempt a case against sellers of "My Wild Irish Rose." If the bloom that the lyricist hopes to take from his girl is not the hymen or maidenhead or—put it down—cherry, I'll eat all the compilations of synonyms. A very dirty thing, that song!

If only for the absence of evidence or the least tatter of it, I do not believe that any word corrupts. Though only the reckless and inconsiderate would abandon all euphemisms on whatever occasion, the fact is that they awaken in mind, often with swollen effect, the expressions they substitute for. At bedrock they appear, or a great many do, as the fearful and gutless and untidy avoidances of essences by obscene imaginations.

Fortunately or unfortunately, my own writings have

never provoked wide attack, but here and there—in Kentucky, New Mexico, Maryland, as I recall, and, so help me, Montana—pious vigilantes have demanded that they be removed from required reading lists and taken out of libraries. Their target nearly always was *The Big Sky*, though one group insisted that *The Way West* be shot down, too. I can't report in detail on the outcomes of these high-minded endeavors. I haven't followed them. And in only one case, on an appeal from a beleaguered librarian, did I do so much as write a letter of defense.

A writer makes a poor witness for himself. Let others testify for him.

:::::::

10

:::::::

I covered the sessions of the Kentucky Legislature first with fascination, then with disillusion and boredom. One session came to be like another. Faces changed, that was all, not mood or manner or matter. Most purposes, it seemed to me, were small-gauge and nearly all leadership was impotent. I developed the feeling of fixity in deportment and time.

Some issues faded out, to be sure, like one to prohibit the teaching of evolution, which I encountered first in 1928. It was pushed, of course, by men who had not evolved very far. And—I have exaggerated—some things were important, if not always by specific legislation, then by attitudes toward them. Successively, Kentucky was under the domination of the railroad interests, the coal-mining interests and the horse-

racing interests, the so-called Jockey Club. Largely it freed
itself from each of these.

Yet Kentucky legislators yammered incessantly over
subjects often unimportant, through motives seldom unselfish. They passed piddling and unenforcible and indefen-
sible bills. Members of House and Senate and administration
accused one another—and still do—of dereliction, misfea-
sance and malfeasance, and the charges were often justified.
It was just as much a mark of the tribe that malefactors
seldom were pushed into court. The wind of political scandal
blew almost without pause, set in motion more often than not
by that excellent newspaper, the *Louisville Courier-Journal,*
which fought and still fights lonely fights for good government and often loses elections, perhaps because of an elec-
toral pride in keeping Kentucky politics down to the poet's
designation of "the damnedest."

Kentucky is a various state. Many of its counties are
paupers. A very few are rich. The stream of civilization has
left eddies of poverty and that ignorance which, through its
nature, becomes assertive and all-knowing. Culture comes up
against a man who carries a pistol. Progress stumbles on the
King James Version of the Bible, every word of which was
authorized by God, not translated by fallible scholars, not
first given to the world so recently as 1611.

I often wondered why good men—there were some of
them—kept running for Senate or House. The rewards
seemed so meager, the frustrations so great. The explanation
may lie in Kentucky's love of politics, a love that results in
election piled on election and keeps partisans whooping and
voters trotting to polling places.

It would be easy for an observer of any legislative session to lose faith in our processes, easy, that is, if they
weren't better than any alternative known, and easy if from

the welter there did not emerge men of force and integrity. Though I am not captive to a name, Republican or Democrat, there comes first to my mind United States Senator John Sherman Cooper. I came to admire him, in 1928, I think it was, when he was a fledgling representative from Somerset. He has remained his own man successfully, if to the discomfiture of the patronage-seeking, back-room Republicans who tarnished the party. Which makes you think the electorate can't be so dumb after all.

I came to know the men who made headlines. Count among them Alben W. Barkley, the later Veep, for whom I did not feel that admiring affection that many Americans eventually did. I knew from the earlier records how easily he had bent to political winds. Of all the politicians I knew, the most interesting, if not the best, was Albert Benjamin Chandler.

He was a poor boy with gall. He was a master of corn, who called people by name from the platform and sang "Sonny Boy" to rapt country audiences. With his original stake of the red sweater and the five-dollar bill, which he often mentioned, he was Horatio Alger. He was *Strive and Succeed*. And for his first eighteen months as governor he was one of the very best governors Kentucky ever had.

He seemed then to be a man both of courage and conviction, if also of cheap ingratiation. The conviction disappeared for me when, after a year and a half as governor, he undertook to unseat Barkley, then U.S. senator. Both men used methods and recruited forces in ways less than admirable; but Chandler was the big disappointment. Through wholesale state employment of weed-cutters and others who performed no discernible function other than to fatten his vote, he forsook the professed policies that had helped make him governor.

I reported my disillusion to Mary Lizzie, who by way of advice to Happy Chandler quoted Shakespeare's Cardinal Woolsey: " 'Cromwell, I charge thee, fling away ambition: By that sin fell the angels.' "

Two giants, no longer candidates, enlivened the political scene when I first arrived in Kentucky. They were A. Owsley Stanley and Edwin P. Morrow. No other pair in men's recollections so delighted the voters. Stanley, then Morrow, won the governor's seat, and Stanley went on to the United States Senate.

They ran for governor in 1915, Stanley as the Democratic nominee, Morrow the Republican, and stumped the state in debates whose echoes still ring. Personal friends and political foes, successors to the mellifluence and orotundity of a handful of Kentucky orators, they brought to the hustings not only sonority but a generosity of wit that made attendance more than worthwhile. Barkley, the Veep, exponent of heightened language and funny insertion, shrank by comparison. He wasn't a giant. No one else was either, and none is today. We shall not see and hear such giants again. Blame the goggle or squawk box or both if you will. They do stand in the way of regeneration, but the old-time manner and talent were going out before electric transmission came in. Tastes changed. The ear dulled, the eye dimmed, blood got tired.

Legend has grown up about the two. What is told for fact may in fact be fiction. What surely is fiction, because claimed as an occurrence on too many platforms, is a story nonetheless apposite. The contestants, it seems, had been hitting the bottle together before exhorting a crowd. Fraternally they went to the courthouse where Morrow, by custom the opening speaker, began his pitch. Toward the end of it

Stanley got sick, so sick that at its conclusion he had no choice but to stagger to the rear of the platform and vomit. An irretrievable circumstance—for all but Stanley.

"Ladies and gentlemen," he is supposed to have said as, shaken, he commenced his address, "I beg of you to excuse me. Every time I hear a Republican speak, I have to throw up."

Though this story surely is an invention, no doubt can dilute the accounts of their friendship or conviviality. In a letter to me years afterwards Stanley said, "We fought mightily but ate and drank like friends."

Stanley won the race by just 417 votes. A history of Kentucky edited by Judge Charles Kerr, a Republican, comments plaintively, "it was said by many that this was not a correct tabulation of the vote and did not express the vote as it had actually been given." As if any election in Kentucky were completely honest! No such complaint accompanied the tally four years later when, with Stanley risen to the Senate and taken from direct contention, Morrow was made governor by a margin of 40,000 votes and more.

When I came on the scene, both spoke for their parties. They were party symbols with old gifts of tongue and wit and theater. But it isn't for these later years they are remembered. The stories told of them are older, dating from their hassles on the hustings to and including Morrow's second race for governor. A couple will suffice.

Somehow in debate there rose the subject of international relations. Morrow criticized the national administration. In his rebuttal, quoted here though paraphrased, Stanley stated:

"When Ed Morrow talks about the foreign policy of the United States, he reminds me of a duck paddling about on the placid bosom of a bottomless lake, drawing two inches of water and serenely unconscious of the fathomless depths beneath him."

In his second campaign Morrow attacked Stanley's record as governor. One of his targets was a textbook that Stanley's appointees had approved. Morrow charged that it was full of errors in grammar. He declared that the Democrats could not escape responsibility for foisting a linguistic monstrosity on the innocent school children of Kentucky.

Stanley's retort, here quoted exactly from his kept records, impeached the witness, saying of Morrow's own language:

"Unrelated nouns in open concubinage are crowded into the same sentences, and poor bastard pronouns wander aimlessly through a wild wilderness of words, vainly seeking their lost antecedents, whom they resemble in neither gender, number nor person."

Morrow's gibes largely are lost, remembered for effect rather than phrase. One reason may be that he seems seldom to have put them on paper. It was unusual for him to write out any part of a speech. He just got up and spoke, relying for rejoinder and substance on what was in him.

But one gets a taste of his antique oratory in a paragraph from a tribute he paid to Kentucky, and one can imagine how he played on the theme with his rich and practiced voice, with his schooled sense of theater.

"First begotten of the womb of the Union," he said of the state, "first nurseling at the ample breast of the motherland, she will be the last to desert or dishonor her. To tell the full story of Kentucky's gifts to the life and progress of the Nation; to recount the lofty deeds or give the names of her distinguished sons, is impossible in the brief time now allowed. We can only sketch the mountain peaks of her influence. During the years of her terrible struggle for existence, even before her entrance into the Union, her hardy sons and noble daughters were leading the vanguard in the march of the Nation's progress. Leading in that march of civilization started by Boone and his companions when they threw themselves beyond the walls of the Appalachians and through the gaps of the Cumberlands, and which was to lead on beyond the Missouri across the Western prairies, 'beyond the frowning barriers of the Rockies, down to the lapping waves of the Pacific, where now teeming cities light their lamps by the setting sun ere it sinks to rest in ocean's outstretched arms!' Ah, pioneers of Kentucky! Ah, wilderness road! crimsoned with blood, golden with romance and legend, your story will be told as long as history finds a pen, or truth a tongue. Boone! Kenton! Harrod! Whitley! Logan! Your moccasined feet have left forever their imprint on the shores of time."

Corn, artfully and heartfully handled, turns into bourbon.

A man can't live in foolish fear and count himself complete.

For thirteen years, from 1923 to 1936, I had gone on in terror of utterance in public, and, more and more, because of it, had felt insufficient and less than whole. Public appearance! The mere request that I speak, even though the date was distant and attendance likely to be small, shot me chockfull of adrenalin, and I'd advance some tremulous excuse.

That fear had entered me, it seemed, all of a sudden. In 1923 I was president of my faternity, and we were initiating not only pledges but honorary candidates picked from the faculty, and I was called from a sick bed to preside. Midway through the ceremony I came apart. My muscles twitched beyond control. My voice wavered up and down the scale. My wild heart choked me. The whole world didn't hold enough air for my lungs. Somehow my panicked parts quaked to the finish and I finished collapsed.

I told myself at first I had been undone by illness, that alone. I hadn't. Reaching for reasons, dwelling on my humiliation and perhaps others to come, unwittingly I fed my fear, and I came to understand that a spark can't start a fire in the absence of combustibles.

Soul assessors, if they've read what I have written, may apply their calipers to id and ego, as one did after I had met the enemy repeatedly and knew, however dread the fight, that I could down him. He found I was too close to good adjustment for any help from him. Psychiatry allows wide tolerance.

But, little as I know of diagnosis, I can see the fraternity of examiners thinking, drawing first upon themselves, thinking of the personal problems that dictated their profession—thinking of patrism and matrism, of stern father and fond mother and of identification with one or the other, thinking of Thanatos and Eros, thinking of shame culture, guilt culture, fear culture and of the various and damaging ways that biological urge bursts the bottle of denial. Conclusion: Anxiety neurosis if not, indeed, occasional hysteria and perhaps incipient dementia. Nature, balked face to face, exerts its revenge.

Moralists as to sex will attack the analysis. Let them. I am not the first to find that moralists have dirty minds. They live preoccupied with carnality, obsessed through indulgence or rejection. Shaped by young circumstance, unfamiliar with the turns of history, deceived by excisions, additions, amendments and tortured constructions of writ, they stand dedicated or stricken on ground they don't know to be shaky.

Scholars say our times are permissive, and no doubt they're right, but sometimes I wonder.

A wanton society I wouldn't want, but I'd welcome a more liberal and rational one, one in which fears about the here and hereafter weren't employed to discipline sex.

These are later reflections. First in my thoughts back there in 1936 was my cowardice.

It was time to act, if ever I did. The necessities of newspaper work had added a bit to assurance. I had a baby son, and I didn't want him to grow up knowing his old man was chicken. And there was my wife, Harriet. Credit much of what followed to her. She regarded my affliction with some amusement, for she thought I could do anything if I set my mind to it. But there was sympathy in her, too, and encouragement and determination for me.

With much trepidation, then, I set out to organize a group of men stricken like me, to form a club for the flustered and fearful who'd address one another in the supporting knowledge that the weakness of one was the weakness of all. Care was required here. We wanted no man of composure, though we took in a few finally.

Five cowards besides me showed up at the first session —the county agent, two farmers, a university student and a fellow newspaperman. Even in that small company, exaggerated in importance by us because it was a company and had a purpose, we found public speech difficult. After all had taken their poor turns at it, we discussed recruitment and rules. The beginning rules were just two: We would meet once a week; every member had to speak at every meeting.

In a moment of inspiration, while we searched for a name, Julian Elliott came up with the perfect one—the Lexington Speakeasy Club. To this day it has operated without interruption.

We had to turn away applicants finally, after the roster had increased to thirty. More than that many made the meetings too long. In the number were one or more doctors, attorneys, insurance salesmen, utility-company employees, workers in banks, architects, accountants, business executives, oil men, farmers and students—men of diverse interests and contrasting income, all allied against a common infirmity, of which by agreement I was the foremost example.

We groped for profitable programs. We scheduled debates, impromptu and prepared and extemporaneous speeches. We tried to get emotion into recitations of the alphabet. We tried heckling and unforeseen switches of subjects. A speaker on an impromptu assignment might be halted after he'd got a bite, say, on "Indian Summer" and shunted to "Tinsel," then told to return to the former. Experience recommended a third rule: Except for his first effort no man could discuss his business. The choice was too easy and frequent, and the expositions bored the bejesus out of the audience.

As we groped for programs, so we groped for aids to assurance. We found, not from William James, that the physical pretense of courage helped to create the reality. From somewhere we took the tip that a coin clasped hard in the hand slowed down the heart. Of all undertakings impersonations produced the least pressure, presumably because in a sense a man got out of himself and so escaped personal and naked exposure. Beginners gained poise from playing a part. A great encouragement was the observation, made after a few of the fearless had penetrated our ranks, that the man without fear never got off the ground. Absence of adrenalin surely. We were bolstered besides by the proof that if a speaker didn't sink in his first minute or two, he was assured of less anxious sailing. With the accretion of confi-

dence, as an aid to the ultimate aim and a test of achievement, we ruled that no seasoned member was to decline an
outside invitation to speak if he had interests appropriate to
the occasion.

Confessions of fright eased the falterers—which may
help to account for "Unaccustomed as I am..." We discouraged the practice, except in amusing and apposite instances, for it made for feeble beginnings. Yet many a time
later on, speaking to this group or that, I have used to illus-
trate my plight a story that strengthened me and may bear
telling again.

In the days of the WPA a new school arose in a mountain county of Kentucky. The townspeople arranged a dedication. To speak for the students they chose the high-
schooler highest in grades. A crowd dismaying in size packed
the new auditorium. There came the boy's turn to speak. He
approached the lectern stiff with terror and, speaking over
his quaver, uttered the first of his memorized words. "Ladies
and gentlemen, do you realize that less than half a century
ago the site of this schoolhouse was a howling wilderness?"
There he went blank. For a long and fearful minute he stood
dumb. He repeated the question, hoping by repetition to
slide into the prepared pattern of his address. He didn't.
The painful silence fell again, longer than before, but he was
a brave lad, if scared, and again he went back to beginnings.
"Ladies and gentlemen, do you realize that less than half a
century ago the site of this schoolhouse was a howling wilderness?" He paused for the third time, then ended pause and
speech together: "And I wish to hell it still was."

At the outset I'd wondered how many men would enlist.
How many were troubled and sat uneasy and silent at public
gatherings when they had something to say? How many
dodged when invited to speak? Enough to constitute one little

club? The eventual evidence, exhibited both at home and later afar, dumbfounded me. Our membership pushed to its practicable limit. Unable to get in, male students at the University of Kentucky formed a club of their own. Townsmen established a third. A group of women organized. *The Reader's Digest* got wind of us and asked me for a letter setting forth our aims and procedures. It sent an editor down to observe operations. His piece appeared in 1940. Afterwards I found how common and far-flung was our frailty. Inquiring letters came from every state and from countries halfway around the world. *The Reader's Digest* had paid me $300 for my letter, which I considered pretty handsome, but in replying to correspondence I spent much of that on stationery, postage and a mimeographed list of procedures that I enclosed. Clubs shaped after ours sprang up East and West, one of them in Manhattan where a good member, possibly with an eye on gainful potentials, offered to put up $5000 toward the cost of incorporation and increase. In the feeling that money would sully design, we turned him down.

Why this fear of men in groups, I asked myself. Why this fear so deep and general? Surely, even under analysis, few men could uncover reasons as cogent as I thought were mine. What of the Latin nations? Not a letter came from them. Who ever saw a Latin frozen or unstrung? Religion can't account for the contrast. As Catholics, Latins, if obedient, suffer checks in sex as sore as those imposed on fellow believers elsewhere, as sore as those imposed on submissive fundamentalists of other doctrines.

Such musings are beside the point. Bit by uneasy bit, we progressed. We found courage if seldom whole assurance. We learned that victory was not conquest. There would always be the enemy, not by sudden magic to be overthrown, never to be extirpated, but by clash on clash to be reduced and in each engagement mastered. So at last, if not delivered from my devil, I could face him down; and I could face up to my wife and my child and myself.

Thinking back to the club and its benefits, thinking of the young men in modest positions now promoted to important places, thinking of the social influence of good men made vocal and of the increased ease of even man-to-man exchange, I don't and can't poke fun, as many do, at Dale Carnegie courses and Toastmasters' clubs. Shallow perhaps. I don't know. Profit-making, to be sure, but surely not all the profit accrues to their conductors.

I have saved for the last one part of Speakeasy procedure. Each meeting had its critic, appointed by the program chairman. Sometimes the appointments were good, sometimes not, but we counted them good for us, good or bad.

It happened one night that the chairman appointed as critic a man of considerable worldliness and little reserve. To a member as mild as milk he assigned for impromptu delivery the chestnut, "My Most Exciting Experience."

Once, the man said, he had gone to Berea, Kentucky, and fallen in with young college folk, and under a bright moon they had all climbed to the top of a hill and struck a fire and warmed wieners and consumed them in buns and eaten such other fare as the students had brought. The boys were mannerly, he said, and the girls correct and attractive. Later, all sat on the ground and sang songs and still later marched down the hill, where he had to take leave of them. That was his most exciting experience.

Jumping to his feet, our critic cried, "Good God! Haven't you ever had a fight in a whorehouse?"

: : : : : : :

12

: : : : : : :

My first book—that virginal try at free-lance pro-
fessionalism—was as unfulfilling as are most virginal break-
throughs in whatever pursuit. In the absence of entire evidence I can't say it is the worst book ever written, but I've
long considered it a contender. Hard-cover publishers put it
out under my title, *Murders at Moon Dance*. A soft-cover
house renamed it *Trouble at Moon Dance*. Under any name,
the thought of this trash troubles me. When I see it dis-
played on paperback racks, where it somehow survives, I
turn away.

Two or three inadequate things can be said about if not
for it. I needed the $400 that was paid to me outright in lieu
of all earnings except a half share in subsidiary-sale money,

if any. Second, a writer must write a first book; he can't begin later on. Finally, I like to think the example may encourage young writers to push on despite their first efforts.

It was in 1936 that I vowed to write it. Mother was ill, so ill that she had gone to the Mayo Clinic at Rochester, where I went to be with her. There the staff determined in a half day what Montana practitioners hadn't been able to determine in months. She had cancer. Inoperable case. Prognosis negative.

Nevertheless, with that insistence on life that is the hope and sometimes despair of the layman, the diagnosticians prescribed x-ray treatments. The staggered series required a week or ten days to complete.

The hours were long and sad beyond saying. With false cheer I helped her to her appointments, telling her I believed I could see an improvement already. I brought her back. We talked, but never at length; she hadn't the vigor for long conversation. The day would wear itself through, and the uneasy night. With so little to do, I waited the crawl of the clock, hanging to the last fraction of hope that time would tick out a miracle.

But she was being eaten up by this monstrous evil called carcinoma, consumed by it in head and breast and limb, and not knife nor ray nor prayer could exorcise it. (For its origin I'm disposed to blame a dentist who fitted her with faulty dentures without which she wouldn't let herself be seen.)

It would have been easier for me, I think, had she shown signs of fear or self-pity and thus permitted me to weep with her. It would have been easier had I not realized that, if she had any fears, she kept them from the surface, thinking thus to spare me. She must have known she was dying, whether or not the prognosis had been revealed to her, but she stayed calm and almost light of manner and talked of our fine family. Just once or twice—and never with a quaver—did she touch on the chance she'd have to leave us, and then it was to add how blessed she'd been in having had so many happy years. She was sixty-three.

In that time of waiting, day and night, I tried to drug myself with gun-and-gallop and whodunit books. I could write, I told myself finally, as well as these writers; and there must be money, which I needed, in such stuff. What about a mystery and cow-country myth in combination? So far as I could recall, the two had never been blended. All right. I'd blend them. I promised myself to, thinking somehow that a published book, by mere publication, would constitute a last tribute to Mother and maybe boost my bank balance besides.

I put Mother on a Pullman of the westbound Empire Builder at St. Paul. I said goodbye and kissed her briefly and turned fast and went away, not fishing out my handkerchief till I was out of sight.

But the night before had been good, or better than other nights we'd had. We put up at a St. Paul hotel, a shabby place but handy to the station, and I went down and bought a flask for easement and brought it to the room. To my astonishment Mother said she just did believe she'd try a little whiskey. It was high time and past time, I thought, and poured two drinks and presently another two, and in that good release, in those moments of invulnerability to slings and arrows, we talked of Choteau days, and we laughed without forcing laughter, and Mother recalled an experience with Old Fox.

We youngsters had persuaded Father, who knew the book was junk, to read aloud *Black Beauty*, that story of a steed grievously abused. One of the abuses was the blinkers on the bridle that blinded the poor horse to goings-on at sides and rear. Old Fox's was a blinkered bridle. We hadn't thought before, but now we knew how much he suffered, and one Sunday, at our pleading, Father cut the cruel things off and harnessed up the horse. We all got in the buggy. Father clucked for action, and Old Fox started for the gate. Then he looked back and saw he was pursued. With a terrified snort and a great burst of wind, he hit his best stride in one jump. Once around the little lot he went at a clip not matched before or since. Turning for the second lap, he went too wide and bumped into the fence and broke a shaft. Father got him pulled up, trembling in every tissue, and we dismounted, shaken but unharmed. That Sabbath family ride was the shortest of its kind on record. It was also the end of *Black Beauty.*

We filled in the gaps, Mother and I, that one or the other had left, and we remembered other incidents and were able to laugh at them, too; and as bedtime approached, Mother lifted her glass and looked at what she'd not drunk. "Buddy," she said, "you know how your father and I have felt about drink, but I wonder. Maybe we were too absolute. Maybe, without reason enough, we denied ourselves something."

With her words and that night and goodbye in my mind, I traveled to Lexington, there to take over my job and in off hours to author my book.

Within a month I was bored with what I'd set down and bored more by the whole prospect—the contrived and implausible plot, the knights and knaves, and love too pure for motor impulses to pants and panties. Final tribute to Mother, this cheap lie about life? She might shy at outspoken expression, but she knew shallows from deeps. Publication? Money? Hah!

Two things kept me going at this dreary chore. The first but less important was the feeling that I had to show myself I could finish it. I had to establish self-discipline. The second was my wife's steady confidence.

Before I was through, Father sent word. Please come!

At Louisville I picked up Chick, who was then an Associated Press correspondent, and together, on borrowed money in each case, we flew to Helena, where a car met us.

Father was waiting, and Janie, too, in the old home at Choteau. Mother lay unconscious in a downstairs bedroom. I like to think she recognized us. For an instant she seemed to, and then the cloud rolled in again.

There we were, all of us who were left, and soon there'd be one less. There were Father, his virtues and his faults reduced to greater woe, and Chick, the ever-faithful, and Janie, a grown woman now, whose diapers I had changed in years so long ago.

We went out of the house on the day after Mother's death and took a long walk through the fields. The March afternoon was fair enough. What little snow there was was melting under a benign sun. Already the gophers were poking from their burrows and running frisky after winter's sleep. The crows were back from southern rendezvous, ahead of time for mating. Soon the bare fields and the bare stands of willows would be green again. Even now the signs were showing. Ahead, the new season. Ahead, new love and life and summer sun. Behind me, with the tone of ages in his voice, Father kept saying, "Aye. Yi. 'The years that the locust hath eaten.' "

We were lost, all of us, and Father most of all. Nothing seemed familiar, quite. The remembered pastures, the groves along the Teton, the stone-blue, snow-white lift of mountains we had known, the notch cut deep by Deep Creek in whose canyon we had camped and knifed initials on the aspen trees in years before—these lay or stood aloof, known yet now not comprehended. Things don't change, not things like these, I thought, not thinking here was platitude; the eye of the beholder did.

What speech we spoke was superficial, made light by heaviness, made remote from me not alone by loss but by the re-enactment of those last ugly moments at the bedside. The involuntary bowel movement as the coma deepened. The harsh reach for breath. The wasted face and figure. The mouth open and, with the fatal dentures out, turned in. The unclean, shriveled finish of nobility. Death knew no dignity. That's what undertakers were for—to prettify with wax and paint and powder the wretched residue. And yes, ma'am and sir, the cost of the casket includes all our services.

Aye. Yi. The years that the locust hath eaten.

I went back to Kentucky and finished my damn manuscript.

It knocked around for a long time, going from publisher to publisher. Then E. P. Dutton and Company took it. The book came out in 1943.

I won't deny a certain pride in seeing it in print. It was a pride, though, mixed with unease. Out of final shame I bought up the last hard-cover copies to be had in Lexington.

It is a mystery to me that I still receive dribbles of royalties from soft-cover sales.

13

In 1931, thanks partly to that strong loyalty of Mary Lizzie's, I persuaded to marry me the girl I had wanted to marry for nine years. Thirty-two years later, by common consent, we divorced.

I shan't go into the circumstances other than to say they were not ugly and involved no third parties. Perhaps one of the reasons for divorce is that we expect too much of marriage. Holding fast to a fairy-tale lie, we get wedded with the expectation of living happily ever after. With the exception—if it is an exception and not the rule—that may argue for premarital relationships, men and women marry in the uninformed belief that their hungers and their chemistries equate. They seldom do, and the discovery that they don't results in frustration and offense. And couples change with the destruction worked by the abrasive years. They grow apart. Things break and can't be put together again, not by memories, determination or the forgiveness that doesn't really forgive, or, forgiving, comes at most to a patched-up, hands-off truce. In most of America, divorce laws constitute a reflection on our civilization by demanding the allegation of half-truths or untruths. There is an honest if legally eschewed word and an honest if unhappy condition called incompatibility.

Though they are forever ended, though they were often stormy, I look back on my married years with nostalgia and gratitude. We lived lives of high excitement, my former wife and I. Days were seldom dull. She told me once she had married me out of the promptings of mind, a not sufficient reason for marriage; but without her confidence, without her felt and unoffending pressure, I doubt I would ever have tried my hand outside the newsroom. And she bore us two rewarding youngsters, boy and girl, with whom we shared adventure.

We called the king snake Doctor Ditmars. Only one of the seventeen other reptiles once to be found in our house ever acquired a name. His was Doctor Funkhouser, after the local authority who had identified it for us as a milk snake or cowsucker. The others—the hog-nosed viper, the indigo or gopher snake, the ringneck, the various grass and water snakes—we never got around to naming; their addition to our reptile house left little time for titles.

Besides, other and unreckoned responsibilities kept increasing, until at last we found ourselves the tenders not only of the reptiles but of (1) one white rat, (2) ten inbred and highly nervous mice, and (3) one incredibly warty and lethargic toad.

They all came to be in our house as the result of the fascinated interest of our six-year-old son, Bert, in the excellent plates in Dr. Raymond L. Ditmars' *Snakes of the World.* The pictures of the king cobra, the Gaboon viper, the reticulated python, and all the rest engrossed him at once and at length. Let my wife or me sit down and he crawled into our laps, lugging the book with him. He pestered startled and sometimes uneasy guests with his insistence on joint scrutiny. He asked questions that would have stumped the author.

His enthusiasm seemed good to my wife and me. We thought he might slide easily from boyhood hobby into adult profession, like Naturalist Ditmars himself.

As a consequence, when Bert came into the house one day, clasping in one fat fist the small milk snake later called Doctor Funkhouser, my wife stifled her screams and got a box. We put the reptile in it along with some earthworms it might find edible and congratulated ourselves on our bold exercise in child guidance.

Reading of the mild and friendly nature of the common or chain king, we had one sent from Florida that fall. Doctor Ditmars was mild, all right, and friendly, I suppose, though a snake's capacity for affection is limited. After it became acquainted with us, it seemed to welcome the opportunity of winding its cool cylinder about a warm, bare forearm, from which the alert head stood out, spearing a nervous tongue into the universe.

With early spring, we began to worry lest Doctor Ditmars was hungry. The reptile books said that as the winter torpor wore off he should have a live meal—a mouse or a small rat or another snake. And now our troubles began. Though mice heretofore had specked the pantry shelving and rummaged in the Wheaties, we could not find a one. Our

clever little copper cages—$1.19 each—which we had been
assured would catch mice alive, corroded in basement and
pantry. Despairing of them, we tried old-style spring traps,
thinking to snatch from them still warm and possibly accept-
able, if dying, nourishment. The bait molded on the triggers.

So, in desperation, we got Mousie, the white rat, from
the University of Kentucky Physiology Department. It was
a sleek creature, a mouse-size suckling with pink eyes and
silky fur and inquiring whiskers.

We offered Mousie to Doctor Ditmars once. Rather, I
did, against the eloquent if half-spoken opposition of wife
and son. The snake drew back, hissing, as I introduced
Mousie, and then it squirmed forward and poked its nose
gingerly at the white puff and flung itself back and glided
forward again while a fine tremor agitated the helpless suckling.

Unequal to the spectacle, I joined the family in the
kitchen, and we stood there while the clock tolled off the
forty-five dragging minutes that the reptile books allow for
a snake to prove its hunger, and then we all ran for the cage,
and I believe we cheered, for there was Mousie, still alive.
Suckled thereafter on a medicine dropper, it thrived on the
formula compounded for our eight-week-old baby, Helen.

We should have known better then, but Bert insisted on
more snakes, and my wife and I remained in the throes of
enthusiasm for child guidance; and so we acquired the hog-
nosed viper and the gopher snake and the ringneck and a
dozen or more assorted reptiles that Bert kept bringing in
from the fields.

We learned a good deal about snakes. The king and the
gopher quickly became friendly, or at any rate accustomed
to us. To the last, though, the little cowsucker would coil and
vibrate its tail and strike boldly but harmlessly at our hands.

Until it lost its fear of us, the toothless viper would swell its neck, cobra-like, and feint at us. That threat failing, it would flop over on its back and play dead. It gave itself away if we righted it, for it always turned back over.

Shedding was a process always interesting and wonderful. We watched as the skin faded and coarsened and the eyes dulled and the sight finally was lost behind a milky cap. One day the old garment would tear, and beneath it we could see the fine, new, colorful sheath. At that point we usually helped, drawing the shedding skin away carefully. Bert always was delighted when we got a snake peeled out, for then, he said, it was just as if the pet were brand-new.

We might have continued but for the nutrition problem. The situation was acute before the indigo and the viper arrived. Afterwards it was harrowing. I had ordered a small indigo. The one sent us was not an inch under five feet. A constrictor, it was thick and muscular, obviously a heavy eater. As Bert and I pulled foot after foot of its handsome, lustrous, purple-black body out of the mailing box, I thought despairingly that nothing less than a shoat would satisfy it. It was a calm and gentle creature, with amber eyes and the habit of hissing softly when we handled it.

The instructions said it fed on gophers or rats or mice, of which last-named it would require quite a number. And, of course, they had to be live gophers and live rats and live mice. To the best of my knowledge, no gopher ever inhabited Kentucky. Later, I was to wonder whether a mouse had. We never tried for rats, feeling that an encounter between rat and snake would be too suggestive of the Roman arena for our household. As for the hog-nosed viper, its tastes were different. Its meat was frogs and toads, *live* frogs and toads.

No one who has not awakened morning after morning knowing he must have a live mouse by night, no one who has not driven himself out into the barren grass to look for a toad, can know the burden that settled on our house. We trapped and we searched and we searched and we trapped. We kicked through the fields and set cages in garages and tool houses and even in the rodent-infested county jail; and we offered boys ten cents for each mouse or frog or toad delivered alive.

The results were meager. We caught a mouse or two, but always in spring traps that killed them. One was still warm, however, and we managed to get the king snake to take it by agitating it slyly with a stick. Out shopping, my wife snatched a half-dead mouse from a grocery cat, to the damage of her reputation for sanity. We got one toad, too, a pensive and virtually stationary thing which cried so piteously as it started down the viper's eager gullet that we ran and rescued it.

At last we wired to Florida: "Ship immediately two dozen mice, one dozen toads."

The mice arrived a few days later, twenty-four of the most peculiar rodents ever assembled. Some had ticks and some ran crazily in circles. Some were brown, some were black, some were white, and some were parti-colored. You had only to look at them to know they were at the wrong end of a long line of inbreeders and miscegenators. One and all, they won such a tender concern from Bert that we got only fourteen of them to the snakes, and those only by stealth.

It took the toads much longer to arrive, but up the walk, at last, came the expressman.

"Lady," he said to my wife, holding the parcel away from him, "this here box is for you, but I don't think you want it."

He added, "It like to stunk me off the truck all morning. Something's mighty dead in here."

Our enthusiasm had run out to the last reluctant drop by now—my wife's and mine, that is. Bert was eager as ever, except that a proposed trip to Montana had given him another and more immediate interest.

Eventually we decided to give the king and the gopher to the University Zoology Department. The white rat went back to Physiology. Doctor Funkhouser, the hog-nose, the ringneck, and the garters were turned loose. The last fantastic mouse sickened and died. The toad we set out in the grass and he faded imperceptibly into the yonder. For reminders of our project we had the empty cages, plus the following enduring bits of wisdom from our observations:—

1. Once you can bring yourself to lay hand on a snake, any extravagant fear of it is likely to disappear.

2. There is nothing like a snake in the house to keep callers from interfering with your homework.

3. It is hard to catch a mouse alive.

Had our various pets been contemporary tenants of our premises, we would have had a small zoo. In addition to the snakes, the rat and the toad, we acquired at one time or another a box turtle that liked to be set in a corner in front of a piece of banana; a fledgling duck that learned to snap flies off ceilings when we held it up to them; a rabbit that grew as big as a burro and loved to eat chicken bones as well as the nap on a new rug; an albino gopher; an ornery yellow-headed parrot that had learned through prior exposure to baby-cry so pitifully that at first we ran to its cage to see what was the matter, only to be challenged by its tearless, reptilian eye; a Boston terrier and two dachshunds; three infant skunks that we eventually had to release because no veterinarian would disarm them; one tawny, half-wild alley cat that disappeared in the mysterious way of tomcats. And a dyed Easter chick that grew into a White Leghorn pullet.

Came time for the summer tour to Montana, and all our charges had died or been distributed or set free except for one dog, which we would take with us, and the pullet, which we assuredly wouldn't. No problem, though. A neighbor grew chickens. We tossed our bird over his fence and rolled away. But the pullet, never having been introduced into poultry society, was upset by the reduction in status and flew the coop. We learned that much on our return.

As the weeks drifted on, we kept hearing from distant neighborhoods about a white chicken that was being chivvied by dogs and chased by children. No connection, of course.

But about six months later a white chicken roosted hard by our premises. It let me pick it up, a weightless bundle of torn feathers and skin drawn tight over bones otherwise bare. As if it had come home to die, it died.

But I know a chicken has no sense.

There sticks in my memory the little bitch of a dachshund named Coney Island Hot Dog the Second, which our girl child had picked out of a litter. I see them, two little creatures together, and Helen is dressing Coney in doll clothes. Coney submits with the gentle and patient trust that marked her all her life and, dressed, she puts on a parade, for there is a clown in her; and Helen calls everyone to see and then picks her up and sits down and strokes her and tells her what a good dog she is.

Pictures.

Springs come, and summers, and again the maps are out. Which way this year to Montana? It is as if we are already rolling the miles, away from school and work and congestion and fret, back to space and sky and the adventures that mean composure, back to the clean streams and the trout, to the deer that lift anxious heads from the wild grasses as we travel dirt roads, to the bare lifts of buttes and the blue lifts of mountains, to Black Bess or Old Blue or whatever horses this year may take us by wilderness trails into the good lonely wilderness, back to the small town of virtual origin, to the ranch owned by Tom Larson, my father-in-law, and Grandma, who love us all and are loved. Each day good and each one fresh.

And now we are rolling, on through Vincennes, on across the wide rivers; and the country opens and the traffic thins, and elation rides with us.

It is noon, and we are somewhere in Wyoming, unknown miles from nowhere, lost in high sagebrush, except for the brutal, black cut of the road that loses itself in distance, except that to the west and north the Wind River Mountains rise with the uncertain beauty of a mirage. We stop to have lunch on the provisions that Harriet, as usual, has thought to provide. Our small daughter gets from the car, there in the sage, there with a sandwich and a cup of milk in her hand, and she says, gesturing to the splash of milk, "Father, this is beautiful. This is the most beautiful country in all the wide world."

For this moment, in our close company, with the sage fragant and the western sky too distant for thought and the mountains too distant for belief, it was as she said, the most beautiful country in all the wide world.

The gentle autumn of Kentucky, April in color, the long, lazy, sweaty evenings of summer. There are young cries in the backyard, for our children are growing up, as are the boy and girl who belong next door, the offspring of Tom and Beth Clark. Tom saunters over, a mixture of muscle and mind and ambition and worriment. According to season, we pass footballs for the young fellows to catch or bat fungoes to test them. Or Beth comes over and tries her Baptist faith against my unbelief, neither winning. The little girls have birthday parties and get decked out for Sunday school, with no encouragement from me, and are lovely in the way that only little girls can be. Dan and Ethel Bowmar come lazing up the street, and we laugh, thinking of the time he worked for a patent-medicine company which guaranteed its product to remedy all manner of ills. Important in its recipe was alcohol, and on occasion in those earlier Prohibition days Dan would snitch a quart or so, make bathtub gin and treat us all. Whether it was because of these petty pilferings we do not know, but a whole carload of the panacea froze solid in a North Dakota blizzard. Cecil and Leola Carpenter wander down the street to our place, and, according to our interests, we talk of old guns and old furniture and refinishing, and Cecil assists my boy and me in manufacturing a small, three-wheel, buckboard automobile which, accommodating two, really runs and runs like hell around the U of Tahoma Road and Shady Lane. Or Joe Jordan shows up and entertains us oldsters with his bare-bone stories: "Did you hear about the two queer judges who tried each other?"

Rich times. Children we were proud of. Friends, good and outrageous friends, we were proud of, too. Memories.

It was all just yesterday.

Early in 1938 I began to read about a Nieman Fellowship program that Harvard University would institute in September. That year and each year thereafter twelve newsmen, more or less, would be chosen for in-service exposure to faculty members and library. The lucky men, granted leaves from their jobs, would draw checks roughly equal to suspended pay. They would have free choice of pursuits, excluding actual courses in newspapermaking, which the school didn't offer; Harvard, bless it, wasn't and isn't in thrall to vocational training. And, fortunately, the Nieman bequest that was to finance the fellowships wasn't rigid in its wording. The million and a half dollars, the will stated simply, was to be used "to promote and elevate the standards of journalism."

A free year of free study! Back to campus and classroom after long absence! Association with such scholars as I'd never dared hope to meet! A library such as I'd never seen! Reading to bridge the acknowledged gaps! I applied.

I didn't expect, or perhaps even want, to quit newspaper work then. I wanted to know more and to improve in my occupation through knowing. I felt the need of exposure, of the challenge of ideas and attitudes foreign to my Bluegrass and Montana provinces. A man just once in Manhattan, never elsewhere on the eastern shore, never anywhere much except in the West and high South, could do with some cultivation.

I can't remember why I thought I might qualify. I had been a deskman for a good many years, and deskmen, good or bad, are largely anonymous, strangers to recognition for want of bylines and circulation in public. My number-one item was the small honor of having had a feature story included in an anthology called *Headlining America*, issue of 1937. The subject was the 1936 inauguration of Happy Chandler as governor.

In further support of my application to the Nieman Foundation I could say only that I managed a considerable staff, wrote frequent editorials and had instituted a good many public-service campaigns. My book, could it have been counted as an asset, at the time still hunted for a publisher.

The committee on selections wasn't impressed, nor was I disappointed, though I did wonder about the appointment of one Louis M. Lyons, a newspaperman from Boston, a city not celebrated for high standards of journalism. In self-protection I had learned not to link chance with certainty and had tendered my bid only in the still-held conviction that if a man keeps an iron in the fire some day a maverick will be marked with his brand.

Six years passed. During them war burst on the nation. Mother died. A daughter was born to us. Outside activities, some war-connected, took more and more of my time. Work remained taxing. I came down with encephalitis.

Sleeping sickness, most people called it, but I couldn't sleep for the ache in my head, for the riot of thought, for the prospect of more spinal taps, those needlings right at the seat of life, that kept my swollen brain from bursting its cap.

Later, as advances were reported in medical science, I diagnosed my disease as equine encephalitis, transmitted by a mosquito that had sucked blood from one of three stricken horses on Tom Larson's ranch, which I had visited on vacation the summer before. For ten months the germ had bided its time.

Two weeks in the hospital, I thought as I left it, and soon back to work. But over the weeks I found I couldn't work for much more than a half hour at a time. My neck kept letting or drawing my head down. Home then to my bed and my pillow.

The doctor spoke ominously of residual effects, of Parkinson's disease, for example. I wouldn't want that. Whatever it was, I surely wouldn't. He shook his head and recommended that I go to Johns Hopkins, though it was doubtful that doctors there practiced a therapy unknown to Lexington.

Harriet said no, I wouldn't go to Johns Hopkins. Within less than a week all four of us were on the way to Montana by train.

It was haying time on the ranch when we got there. The horses that had lain almost immobile last summer were back on their feet—but what specimens! Gaunt and listless, glazed of eye, they'd never again carry saddle or harness. Zombies, I thought, looking them over.

Give me a sulky rake and a team, I told Tom, and I'll
help with the haying. He regarded me with doubt and concern but said sure. Some days I could help, some part-days,
that is. Some days I couldn't. Dizziness interfered, or inter-
mittent intercranial pressure that I compared with an ac-
cordion. At the barnyard, undone, I'd survey the three
horses, reduced to the category of canners.

I sound more doleful than I felt. Only in rare moments
did I apprehend death or even permanent impairment. How
could people live and love and languish, how could history be
made and the World Series be played without my awareness?
Here were my old reliables of skull and nerves and members.
They'd get all right. Apart from these conscious assurances,
I had too much bounce for abiding anxiety.

It is curiosity that makes dreadful the prospect of
death. It is the thought of not knowing. Here our own fish-
hook snags us, said John Burroughs, the naturalist, in calm
resignation when he reached seventy. We are thinking from
being and thus extending live sensibilities to the insensible
grave. Dead men don't wonder what's new. Roll on, infinity!

But the snag is a snag until a man ceases to feel it, and
so, save for a relative few who want death not so much as
removal from life, we all dread termination, even those who
foresee association with angels. Angels wouldn't be likely to
subscribe to the *Times.*

More, though cold reason carries him farther, it's next
to impossible for a man to imagine a world without him. It is
made real by his fingers and feet. It exists in his eye. It
wouldn't smell except for his nose or sound if his ear didn't
hear or have taste except for his tongue. Without his awareness, nobody, nothing, a cipher voider than the cipher
atomic warfare could write. Impossible, this barren prospect.
A man goes on his way, often cheerfully, often dejectedly,

but in either case insured against death by essentiality until, late or soon, the policy lapses.

Recognition came to me suddenly after haying was done. It came in an instant one day in September. I knew all at once, and I turned to my wife and announced, "We can start packing. I'm well."

Completely recovered, as my incredulous doctor attested, I returned to my desk, to assignments, colored notes, telephone, daily copy, headlines, makeup, editorials. And I determined to put another iron in the fire.

I would write a second novel, this one about the mountain man in the period from, say, about 1830 through the high years of his rule to about 1843, to the time of his self-wrought ruin. I would tell of the fur-hunters who followed hard on the heels of Lewis and Clark, of men in the molds of Bill Williams, Hugh Glass, Joe Meek, John Colter, Kit Carson, Provot and the Sublettes. By boat and by horse and by foot we'd penetrate, my men and I, the surprised wilderness. We'd trap the clucking, beavered streams and bed down in the wondering parks of the almost-untouched young West; and we'd love squaws and fight Indians and spree big at rendezvous and, broke and sober and satisfied, signal goodbye and ride on to untried, rich rivers, counting good beyond telling this life that our blind lives would extinguish.

With the exception of a couple of antique and artless attempts only one novel was tied to the fur trade insofar as I knew. That was one in a series whose protagonist was Stewart Edward White's Andy Burnett. I had followed Andy's adventures with pleasure and inactive consideration. White told a good and clean and therefore short-of-truth story. Not for me a Sunday-school representation of men mostly amoral, I thought with growing conviction. No bowdlerizing of documented behavior. No heroes, or villains for that matter, who never unbuttoned whether to make water or squaws. Be wholly honest! Get to the whole truth! Live and make live again that unfettered life! Don't heroize, keeping in mind that all heroes are errant and that the mountains counted cowardice the first sin and seldom listed a second!

In size and intent the undertaking seemed wildly ambitious, preposterous in relation to the sum of my credentials. I had written a book, if that counted. I knew a good deal about the physical West and, through unorganized reading of records, something about vanished times there. Through the years I'd assembled a small but select early-Western library, a start for organized research. My interest was real and almost nostalgic. I had spent years in Kentucky and encountered that dark strain so often found in the hill folk who could claim more than one mountain man and now would provide my protagonist. A typewriter sat at home, ignored and sullen. Scant and weak for the venture, there was my muster.

It is difficult for any writer, amateur or professional, to assay the ore he mines. What appears to be gold may be dross. The rich vein may be base. Conceit may have salted his diggings. He works in a lonely and uneasy knowledge that determinations wait on outside assayers.

Or sometimes, especially if he's unseasoned, he may reject valuations that jar his ego. He knows nuggets and veins when he sees them. He can tell precious from base. And the words that he's written, by God, are golden! It is best to leave this prospector alone in the desert with his faithful jackass.

Hard as it is for a writer to judge whether his words are

working, it is harder yet for him to perceive why they're not. He's too close to them for examination and verdict, too sorely kin to all to pass sentence on any. Each pristine expression, every original effort to shape and relate the larger components of story asserts a relative's claim and fights upstart interventions by bastards. Yet somehow he knows that his lines don't do to the reader what he wishes them to. They don't—and they must above all—carry him through a course of experience.

At this point it is time and past time to seek help, to find and impose on that rare and knowledgeable someone who can excite his awareness and focus his confused eye on effect. Apply the seat of your pants to the seat of your desk chair, a sage advised writers, and something will come out. Uh-huh. But what? Prayerful perserverance alone is all too likely to confirm the anchorite in evil practice.

I had no enlightener and small perseverance—two negatives that left me at virtual zero. After writing three chapters I suspected my imagined reader had quit me. I couldn't blame him. My copy stank.

That much was apparent. The reasons weren't. Not even one reason was. Not overwriting, for one. Or journalese. Or the precious insertion of personal wisdom that stood in the way of the story. Or long-loved long words. Or declaration instead of evidential suggestion. Or the confinement, not the release, of imagination brought about by adverbs and adjectives. Or lack of imagery. Or wandering viewpoint, if any. To most of these considerations I'd never given thought. Whatever thought I had given to the few was no aid to detection of guilt. Case filed away as unsolved.

Even before this abandonment two old friends were nagging me to do something I'd done before. One of them

was John F. Day, at latest report on foreign assignment
with *Time-Life*, whom I'd lucked into hiring when he came
out of college. The other was the late Paul J. Hughes of the
Louisville Courier-Journal, whose friendship I'd prized over
the years since we met as fellow legislative correspondents at
Frankfort. Both had gone to Harvard as Nieman Fellows.
A rich experience, they swore, rich beyond my imagining.
The contacts! The good conversations! The heady courses!
The general geniality! The books! The opportunity for a
man to draw back and have a cool look at himself! I had to
re-apply, that was all.

To my protest that my age was against me they said
the foundation had raised the limit because younger men
were in service. What if I had tried once and failed? Now I
had a book to my credit and an article in the *Atlantic*. What
was more, what was much more because of their acquaintance
with the authorities, I would have their endorsements.

I applied, and it came about that I was asked to appear
before the selection committee at Louisville; and now for the
first time I began to think: maybe.

There were just two committeemen, if I counted right
while my legs wobbled me into the room. One was Dr. Arthur
M. Schlesinger, Sr., who swam owlish and fearsome with
wisdom. The other was a puff of pipe smoke whose eyes
looked smokily through it. It went by the name of Curator
Louis M. Lyons and announced along a pipestem that the
third member could not be present.

They talked easily, the owl and the smoke, as if to put
me at ease, and shortly transformed themselves into men,
and friendly men at that.

Yet the session was short, too short, I thought, for
an interview, and too casual for consequence; and I left the

room thinking it had been called, probably, as a gesture of courtesy to two former Fellows.

I underrated my references. I must have. The committee approved me.

And that, to use Robert Frost's line, made all the difference.

15

In the fall of 1944 the four of us in the family set out for Cambridge. Our conveyance was an old Nash. The Office of Price Administration in those days of rationing, apparently debating the merits of Harvard and me against the needs of the nation, had been a trifle reluctant to authorize new tires and extra coupons for gas. We got them, though, and we had rented our house and cozened the tenants into keeping our dog; and we rode with that pilgrims' misgiving that keeps asking what arrangement or item has been forgotten.

Two adults and two children, ages five and eleven, in our manifest. What clothes we expected to wear. Such stuff, crammed in the trunk and piled high around us, as temporary households are made of. We were Okies off course but didn't quite qualify as absolute paupers since, for the sake of our five-year-old, Harriet had remembered to throw in a pot. Probably she would have done so in the absence of small fry. Women are more thoughtful than men in these matters, having to go oftener and being less well equipped for undetected al-fresco relief.

We tooled up through the rich fields of Ohio, breathed Wheeling's smoke, traversed Pennsylvania's grand tumble of lowland and mountain and came to New York and rolled on; and the days were sunlit and the leaves bannered with fall, and ahead was adventure, magnetic but in faint moments dismaying.

What good fortune, I thought while we wheeled along on our half-illegitimate tires, propelled by our almost black-market gas. What incredible luck, come my way because younger men were fighting a war to keep me secure. There was the contradiction, there the shrink from the full measure of exultation. How could I rejoice when the man who might have been in my place might at this moment be suffering from hardship or fear or wounds or might already be dead? But without breaks, who succeeds? What talent or industry, even what genius, comes to full flourish without fortuity? These rebuttals are present ones. I wasn't so sure or explicit then. In my rejoicing was just the sobering knowledge that I wouldn't be on my way but for war.

Uneasiness rode with me, more and more as we progressed. This land we rolled through was foreign, remote from all that I knew; and in a return of rural timidity I sensed the touch of hostility. We had little money in pocket or bank. What would my fellow Fellows be like? The faculty? What lay in store for a rube newspaperman? We'd been warned that housing would be hard to find, what with

Cambridge bursting with trainees and technicians and other
war-effort workers. Our single assurance of lodging was two
nights at the Commander Hotel. Then, said the management,
we'd have to get out. We surely would. We couldn't afford
twelve dollars daily.

And afterwards, with two children, one just out of
arms?

By night, by mistake, we took the truck route from Ded-
ham to Boston, too tired for civility, too soiled for the Salvation Army. The Charles River eluded us. So did its bridges.
Where, we kept asking after hunting them out, was the
Commander Hotel? Cantabridgians didn't know. They answered vaguely or negatively in that atonal, unpleasant,
added-r speech of the subways.

We never did get accustomed to that kind of talk. Later
we thought it was funny and grinned when the radio gave us
"The Mere Idear of You." Even today I'm mildly amused
when I hear that non-existent "r" added to a word usually
ending in "a." It is as if, in the equal society of letters,
amends have to be made for the neglect of the eighteenth
one, as in "paak" for "park," by giving it a lift to the
tailgate.

We discovered the Commander at last, thanks more to
exploration than curbside direction, and made camp.

Next morning we walked down to Nieman headquarters
in Holyoke House, talked to Louis Lyons, met what Fellows
were present and learned that the problem of shelter was even
more difficult than we had imagined. There just weren't any
places reasonably close to Harvard Yard, or, if there were,
they weren't family-size and probably not passable anyhow.
The foundation kept combing the town but now had nothing
better to offer than a suggestion that we visit Phillips Brooks
House. Each afternoon at a given hour the people there dis-

tributed copies of a list of lodgings available. No, we couldn't get advance information. The distribution was made at the same time to everybody.

We took a look that same afternoon. In front of the place private cars and cabs were lined up, engines gunned and doors opened. Inside were thirty or more men and women, all wondering, it appeared, where their next sleep was coming from. At the sound of unseen movement a sudden expectation animated them. A door opened, and girls came out, bearing hope, and dealt it to grasping hands. A blind rush for outdoors then, with people attempting to read as they ran. The roar of engines. The squall of tires. Silence. The Phillips Brooks House went to sleep.

"A town we don't know," I said to Harriet. "Cab drivers we can't afford day by day and can't compete with in our own car. This is hopeless."

"So you give up already!" she said, her voice edged. "Then leave it to me."

I was happy to.

She bought and studied a map of the city. For a day or two she toured around in the old Nash, getting her bearings. Then, the boomer, she pronounced herself ready for the daily signal that opened the strip. Before we finally staked out a homestead—no thanks to Phillips Brooks House—she could outrun her rivals, from doorway to vehicle, and outgun and outgame the orneriest cabbies in Cambridge. During those dashes I stayed with the kids in the Commons, a chicken feeding peanuts to pigeons.

That first day was the most forbidding. We had spent one of two nights in the hotel, half of our allotted span. To-morrow at three o'clock would come an end to what was called hospitality but came closer to sufferance. No, the man at the desk said with the cold authority that a full house confers, he wouldn't and couldn't extend our stay. We didn't know how lucky we were to be there even briefly.

Early the next morning Harriet set out on foot and returned tired but happy just ahead of the bouncer. "I found a place," she announced.

"An apartment already!"

Of course not. A single room with two beds. All the same, it had advantages over the gutter.

The house stood on Mellon Street or, rather, collapsed there, a New England example to the prodigal world of the thrifty use of decay. The room did have two beds, one that unfolded and, folded, left floor space for one standee and a half. An incredible population infested the house. Behind each of its numberless doors was a denizen. Some were night-faring and creaked up the steps at dawn like Dracula bound for his coffin.

We got out of there shortly and moved for a month's stay, no more and no less, to an apartment that Harriet had found in a rickety, Brattle Street inn. The floors of this haven defied horizontal convention. From the pole in the fixed north of the parlor they fell away, each on its own. But we didn't fault the place. We had our own toilet!

Our thirty days diminished to twenty, to ten and to five. A slim possibility arose, reported to Harriet by a woman dealer in real estate she'd become friendly with. An apartment on Buckingham Street was about to be vacated. The hitch was that the owner and his wife, who lived next door, hesitated to rent to a couple with children. Immediately beneath the space to be vacated lived two long-time tenants who objected to noise.

Then I learned that the owner was the retired superintendent of city schools, and I put wife and kids in the car and went to call. We had much to talk about, the pensioned schoolman and I, the son of a man in like situation. Harriet and his wife quickly established a friendly ease. The youngsters were mannerly, as I knew they'd be without ad-hoc drilling. The apartment, if we liked it, was ours. Without looking, we liked it.

Home at last. Home for nine months at least. And never once in our time there did the good downstairs couple complain. They even lied to me, once we'd become friends, saying when I apologized for a rather noisy Nieman party we'd given that they hadn't heard a sound.

Another and never-solved family problem was the problem of food. We went hungry in Cambridge that year, went if not malnourished then not well-fed, wanting table items that ration stamps, if we had them, and cash, if we had it, too seldom produced. Meat was hard to come by and harder to cut unless you were a known and favored customer. There was available sometimes an unidentified bird called "fowl," no relation to a chicken. The fishermen had forsaken the sea for fatter earnings in factories. No fish today. Regularly the Faculty Club served horse steak, but the cost of nerving oneself for a cheap piece of Old Paint was considerable, Old Nosepaint being high as it was. We went six weeks without an egg and then had to argue for three. An extra-nice man sometimes would discover a chop if first we put out for a bottle. When he raised the ante to two bottles, we pitched in our hand. A grasping, snarling lot, those Cambridge tradesmen.

But periodically out of the West, out of a West almost untouched by restrictions and shortages, fresh from Tom Larson's ranch would come a couple of turkeys or a half-dozen chickens into which our old friend Nick Vlinker, butcher and rancher, had thrust two or three pounds of butter and as many of bacon; and we'd summon our under- fed friends, and we'd eat, all of us, as if hunger knew no tomorrow.

: : : : : : :

16

: : : : : : :

Nine other men were members of the 1944–45 group of Fellows. A diverse lot by geography, interests and attitudes, they were alike as possessors of uncommon qualifications. Each, as a Rotarian would say, had something to contribute and indeed contributed it. If some of my introductions, about to be made, appear frivolous, they aren't made with any intent to belittle. Often, in warm remembrance, trivial and funny things come first to mind.

Houstoun Waring, editor of the *Littleton Independent* in Colorado, had earned recognition—and has gone on increasing it—as one of the best country newspapermen in the land. But country newspapering involves mechanics in addition to editorial direction, and one day after a Boston

Harbor cruise with the Coast Guard he asked me, "Did you
know that the Coast Guard is the most hazardous occupation
of all?" I didn't. "Yes," he went on. "Coal mining's next." In
class thereafter I noticed how eagerly he jotted down such
little nuggets of fact. From my own rural-shop experience a
picture began to emerge, later to be sharply focused by another question. I saw him there in his shop, and it was paper
day, and before him in a chase was a column of type that,
being short of fixed length, left a hole in the page, and he
ran to the linotype and set the answer to the last question
he'd asked me and with it filled the hole. The answer went:

> Research by experts in the field of animal
> husbandry indicates that a cow of average
> weight drinks forty gallons of water every
> day.

Nathan Robertson, then of *PM*, was so far to the left as
to affront reason. Or so he struck me at first. And he was absolute and noisy in argument. He'd proclaim and shout and
beat on the table. Then he'd turn, as if suddenly conscious of
excess, and a grin would split his thin face, and behind his
glasses his eyes would be misty with friendliness; and you
would know after repeated exposure that here was a man
whose fault, if it was one, was simply that he wished all
people impossibly well. He wanted more for everybody than
could ever be given, yet was far too principled and intelligent for the trap that communism sets for open hearts and
weak minds. Though never winning me over, he made me re-
examine and alter my thinking. In a fit of diabetic dejection
he took his life later and left a hole in mine.

Kendall Foss came from *Time* magazine. He was a hard
one to figure. He was a friend or at least a colleague of
Whittaker Chambers, that later defector from communism,

whose talents he admired while shaking his head in what seemed a rueful perplexity at whatever he knew of the man's philosophy. Sometimes he spoke of communism, sometimes of Naziism, with a degree of approval the rest of us couldn't second. Sometimes he applauded aspects of democracy. His well-informed mind, by far the most intricate and involved to be found in the group, by its very complexity seemed to keep him forever from going beyond second premises, if it allowed him that far. But on the road to inconclusion one recognized a rich and erudite intelligence.

We never got to know the late William H. Clark of the *Boston Globe* as well as we outlanders got to know one another. That no doubt was because he was on his home range and had many friends outside the group, as we didn't. He was a reserved man with a quiet dry wit, a great interest in botany and a solid conviction that lobsters were hardly worth eating unless taken fresh from the actual lobster pot and prepared for the table immediately. The proof was supplied me by a meal at his house. Unlike some or even most of the rest, he was a conservative, a New Englander who, one suspected, had never inscribed his X in the wrong column.

Robert Bordner, on the staff of the *Cleveland Press*, seemed to hold in private reserve a good deal of himself, with the consequence that one never felt quite on close terms with him. Congenial and easy in manner, he still chose on occasion to keep himself solitary, to go alone on unannounced jaunts and to report where he'd been only if questioned. But under the right circumstances he would tell hysterical tales. One of them was about an enormous snake which for weeks he'd kept alive in the news if nowhere else by straight-faced reports of vague sightings, confirming spoor and subscribers' conjectures—all to the titillation of readers, among whom no doubt were some whose imaginations and unsought

connivances animated the monster. At Cambridge he wrote a
tongue-in-cheek roundup of the case and sold it to the *Atlantic Monthly*. It was his appearance, however, that struck a
man first and will remain when memory falters. He had a
merry eye, an eye with a spark in it, and on his lip he cultivated a mustache that would have stampeded a longhorn. He
explained, twirling the waxed ends of it with hands surely
eight inches apart, that its purpose was to impress his identity on those from whom he gleaned news. Possibly he had
other clues for the blind.

There were also—but not also-rans—David E. Botter,
Jr., of the *Dallas News*, Edward Edstrom of the *Louisville
Courier-Journal* and Ben Holstrom of the *Minneapolis Star*.
They were keen newspapermen, and they come sharp to
mind, though their particularities somehow don't suggest in-
dividual paragraphs. Botter went from the *News* to the
Look organization and from there to the teaching staff of
Northwestern University, where he died. Edstrom joined the
Hearst bureau in Washington, where he served a term as
president of the National Press Club. Holstrom quit the
Star in favor of advertising agency work in Chicago and
quit that in favor of small-town newspaper publishing in
Ojai, California.

Charles A. Wagner, last of the nine, requires more
space if I am to tell two stories that stick with me. Wagner
was Sunday editor of the *New York Mirror*, a strange place,
it always seemed to me, for a truly gentle man, for a lover of
music and poetry, a follower of history and later the author
of a book about Harvard. Just as contradictory were a couple of seemingly out-of-character performances. We had had
a seminar, open to visitors, and across from Wagner sat a
Chinese coed, and, after we'd broken up, Wagner took me
aside and told me in high delight: "It's not true, Bud. It's a

myth, that Caucasian idea about Oriental female anatomy. She's regular!" Prankishness or no panties? I never knew. At still another seminar an Australian economist was explaining how Australia under his guidance was managing her wartime economy. The going was difficult, both for him and for us, and at a point where all was to be won or lost with a last heave, Wagner raised a questioning hand. The speaker recognized him. "Mr. So-and-So," Wagner said with outward earnestness, "I've been sitting here wondering. Has Australia ever tried to do anything, anything commercial, I mean, with kangaroo pouches—like making ladies' handbags, for instance?" The Australian stammered, "Not to my knowledge." The knowledge he did have didn't go very far after that.

Whatever we were, wherever we came from, we got along. Arguments never developed into animosities. Differences of interests and tastes were respected. The ages of eight of us helped to make speculative the passes that younger men might have made at other men's wives, and our two juniors, Botter and Edstrom, observed the proprieties.

Over us—with us is better—was Louis Lyons, curator, adviser and friend. He was patient and thoughtful. Knowing Harvard, he knew where and how and to whom to direct us. He put and kept life in the program and hopeful determination in us. He was open to reason but firm in high principle. And, in addition, because he had been and still could be a good newspaperman's model of a newspaperman, our acknowledgment went beyond the mere recognition of official position. Even so, unless we stopped to think, I fear we came to take him as a matter of course, his good offices were so freely and unpretentiously tendered.

My family developed a happy routine. Each weekday we'd set out together on foot, each with his green Harvard bag. Helen and Bert would drop off at Cambridge School, a private institution we'd chosen because parochial politics had made a sour joke of the public-school system. Sometimes Harriet and I went together to class, either at Radcliffe or Harvard, for they worked together in a manner we never tried to comprehend. Oftener, she'd stop at Radcliffe, and I'd walk on to the Yard, there to listen—days and nights and weeks and months mix in memory here—to Payson S. Wild or Herman Finer or Frederick Merk or Kenneth B. Murdock. Or to Alvin H. Hansen or Charles H. McIlwain or John H. Williams or Philip D. Bradley. To Nieman Fellows the whole institution of Harvard was open. The free gold was there to be had, limited only by the size of our pokes.

Men, impressions, old enlightenments shine through the layered years. Fred Merk stands frail with his big watch in hand, telling his class of America's westering in a manner unique, out of a knowledge unmatched; though I don't know it now, I shall borrow from him again and again. Charles McIlwain, almost old enough for retirement, irreplaceable even in imagination, speaks of Stephen Langton, and the centuries of man's struggle for freedom unroll, and here blazes the Bill of Rights. Payson Wild explores natural law and introduces me to the eloquence of Cardozo. Ken Murdock defines naturalism and realism in literature, and I decide I'd rather be a Frank Norris than a William Dean Howells. Phil Bradley lectures on currencies, and I think how foolish was American criticism of Great Britain, which built battleships but had the nerve to plead poverty and paid only a token on her American debt. At Sunday teas at the home of Mr. and Mrs. Arthur M. Schlesinger, Sr., we actually drink tea. We don't need alcohol; the conversation supplies jolt enough. Wherever I am, I'm likely to keep uneasy company with embarrassment, remembering attitudes

taken and editorials typed, and I wonder how many colum-
nists speak, how many editors write with the assurance of
ignorance.

Seminars. Dinner meetings. Passing associations.
Bernard DeVoto, peppery as a south-of-the-border tamale,
reciting with spice and spite the story of Boston's lunatic
censorship. Edward Weeks, editor, step by step laying bare,
with his highly practiced informality, the hoax that suck-
ered the *Atlantic* into buying and swearing by a collection of
Lincoln papers later proved spurious. Harlow Shapley,
astronomer and wide-ranging thinker, prickling us in this
time of international slaughter with the suggestion that
maybe war isn't so bad: consider the American economy, for
example. Morris Ernst regretting the decline in the number
of newspapers, proposing remedies and making sense.
Luncheons at the Faculty Club, where gather Theodore
Morrison, Paul Buck, Alexander Reed Powell, and other no-
tables beyond notation here, who grow to know us and bring
us genially into their talk.

It was all pure luxury and all excitement, an excitement
so high that I fell victim to what the doctor diagnosed as
globus hystericus, a sort of reverse, upper-canal peristalsis
that keeps bringing an imaginary but endlessly swallowed-at
baseball to the throat. Manifestation of an anxiety neurosis,
probably, the doctor said, adding that it was ordinarily a
female affliction and, as if to restore my pride, that medicine
recorded no instance of such distress among Negroes. Then
he looked at Harriet, sitting tense at my side, her hands
working in her lap, and said she appeared more in need of
medication than I did. So both of us went out with prescrip-
tions and, having bought medicine, called by request on
Helen's kindergarten teacher. Little Helen was nervous, the

teacher said; she kept thinking she had to go to the bathroom. For a year at Cambridge, bring tranquilizers.

Luxury, though. The luxury of association with trained
and penetrating minds. The luxury of learning when other
luxuries have shaken into place, when young distractions are
seen as evanescent, have diminished from compulsive to occasional. Lecture hall and seminar and, for research on the
West, a cubbyhole at Widener Library with all its precious
books, and the steps of Widener where I sat sometimes, feeling easy but alive and enlarged. The thought that people
attended and completed school too soon, as I had, and the
right to think, if right it was, that the Harvard staffmen,
depressed by the insolent and glandular omniscience of age
twenty-one, took heart and expanded with the discovery that
what they were and knew and said caught honest hold on
older men. Yes, here, I thought, lounging on the steps one
day as spring stepped out, here could be a way of life if only
the foundation would sentence me to life.

Even Ken Foss surely would join in my conclusion:
Nothing better than a Nieman Fellowship can happen to a
newspaperman.

: : : : : : : :

17

: : : : : : : :

Louis Lyons sat and drew on his pipe, letting go with "Yahs" when he puffed.

We were alone in his office, and I was telling him I wanted to write a book with the American fur trade as its background. I took his monosyllables to be questionable encouragement.

I said, as nearly as I remember, "It's a novel I have in mind, Louis, not a study or history or anything like that."

Through the open door to the front office I could hear Dotty Bevan, Louis' secretary, moving around. I didn't care if she heard. She was our friend.

"I have a few chapters already written, three or four anyhow, but there's quite a lot of research still to do. I think

I could do some research and some writing and still carry on
with my program."

"Yah."

"But, Louis, I need help. I'm not satisfied with the
chapters as they are. I guess what I'm hoping for is a
coach."

"Well," Louis said, coming forward in his chair, "for
research we can get you one of those niches at Widener,
probably on the same floor as the Western Americana. Ted
Morrison in English would be a good adviser, if he has time.
Why don't you see him?"

Ted Morrison turned out to be a pipe-smoker, too.
Pipes seem to have had a lot to do with my fortunes. Bill
Sloane, my first editor, sucked on one all the time. They, the
pipe-smokers, have a great advantage over cigarette-users
and those who count unemployed fingers. What with the in-
cessant lighting of matches, the tamping of fuel, the ream-
ing out and refilling, the striking again of a light and the
slow determination that the cake's baking all right, they create the impression of nerveless, unhurried profundity.

Morrison, a graying man with a fine face, was friendly
enough but reserved, and my words were uneasy, made awkward and halting by his deliberation, by my feeling of judgment held in suspension. He suggested, after he'd got his
pipe satisfied for the fourth or fifth time, that I bring him
the pages I'd written.

The best parts, he said when I saw him later, were the
bits of internal monologue, the passages in which I held
closest to my protagonist. "Internal monologue" was a
phrase new to me. As he went on, I recognized that "best"
was a relative term. Best of a bad lot. My distance from my
character necessarily would vary, he said, but did I want to
divorce him completely, as in my descriptions? Would an

unlettered country boy have thought of "cirrus" clouds and
"sluggard" suns? (God Almighty!)

I had written of the boy, "He was hungry." Well,
maybe all right, Morrison said. Sometimes the quickest and
flattest way of expression justified itself in context, though
it had no appeal to the senses and smacked of authorial in-
trusion besides. But what if I substituted for that dead declaration of hunger: "He thought of the corn dodger and
spring greens Ma might be fixing"?

I make Ted sound blunter and more positive than he
was, and I have shown only a few, ready grains of his seed-
ing. He was always considerate, kindly and tentative in his
words of disturbance and never authoritative, being the first
to admit and announce that if a thing worked, then it
worked, and that was all there was to it.

Lesson One, I thought as I came away from that first
meeting with him. Food for thought. I had a time digesting
it.

All those first weeks with Ted as my tutor were hard. I
would go home after a session and torture my brain. What
was it he meant? What really was wrong, what really had he
suggested? Like other beginners I was impatient with inex-
actitude in a critic and dejected by it. The course should be
easy to chart. A guide shouldn't lose a man in a thicket. I
didn't know then, though I surely learned later, that a
teacher can only suggest, can at best reveal some of the
tricks by which illusion is wrought. The rest is up to the
student, to what there is in him, to his guts and his heart and
his head, all working from the meager base camp that the
teacher has managed to pitch.

When I was most confused and sorest beset, my wife
and I went to a movie. Make it two movies. Boston was
blighted, like towns everywhere, by the double feature. The

second feature, so-called, was bad beyond any imaginable
efforts to worsen it, but we saw it through, munching pop-
corn with no injury to illusion. While the plot unfolded to no
one's astonishment and the dreary dialogue sounded and
actors acted as if their emotions could be communicated only
through seizures, a curtain lifted for me. I had been hamming. Plain, by-God hamming. That was part of what Ted
had been trying to tell me.

A bridge crossed, though not the last one by far. I
needed to understand and to apply other suggestions, advanced with a moderation that only dented my ignorance. I
had to show and not tell, a difficult achievement in any case
and more difficult in the case of a newspaperman who had
spent his life telling. In my characters I had to forget myself. They were my creatures to be sure, but they had to have
a vitality of their own, an independence of me except that, as
the invisible manager, I kept their waywardness in check.
Even that management was demanding, for characters, once
conceived, have a willful habit of jumping the reservation
and must be herded back into the boundaries of story.

Finally I managed to achieve identity with my characters—which meant that I lost my own for the time. I was
at Harvard but wasn't. I was in the young mountains trap-
ping prime beaver. I was frolicking at rendezvous on the
Green. I was peering at distance, watching the dust that
might mean buffalo and might mean Indians. I sat on the
ground, for who wanted a chair? I lived on straight meat,
for who hankered for the fixin's of Eastern tables? I was
alive in unpeopled space and at home with it, counting
buttes and streams and mountain peaks as friends. I wasn't
Bud Guthrie. (The nickname came from my sister, Nina
Bess, who as a toddler couldn't pronounce Bertram.) I was
one of my characters and I was all of them. After I had

finished my manuscript my wife said, "You've come out of the last century, thank God."

Much later, when I was teaching at the University of Kentucky, I said with high authority that identification with character was the first and final feat of the imagination in fiction.

None of us—Ted, my wife or I—had thought of a title for the manuscript, were it to be published. That could wait. It waited a long time. Even after the manuscript was ready for the presses we were racking our brains for one. Finally Bill Sloane said to forget it. Send him some autobiographical notes instead. In the notes I mentioned my father's first day in Montana, when he had stood under the big sky and exclaimed, "By George, I'm free." Sloane wired me congratulations on my title, *The Big Sky*—but it was he who found it.

Once I had seen that movie in Boston, the hardest days were passed, not the hard days of hard work, not the hard days of more learning, but of the confused days of the dark, of blind isolation in ignorance. I had established a beachhead, small as it was and might ever be, on the great island of fiction.

And now things were different with Ted. Reading my copy, he laughed at passages I had worked to make funny and held tight or nodded where I wanted him to. A light would come to his eyes, and there was help in his heart, mine to draw on, and he would say, "Good, Bud, good!" And his words were benediction and benzedrine.

So well did we nick—a horseman's expression for a happy combination of blood—that a beginning word or two from him was enough, both then and later when I was sending him chapter after chapter by mail, to make enlargement unnecessary. Sure, sure, I would say to myself after the first words. Why couldn't I have seen that for myself?

I have already spoken of breaks.

The Nieman program was great, but to me it had a blank in it. Here we were, all of us, reading, listening, studying, passively hopeful of enlarging our calibers. But where was the practice range? Where the means to rebore and sight in the tool that we shot with? The figure is throwing me. Where and how could we learn to be better writers? Newspaper copy, with bright exceptions, was notoriously dull, subject to misconstructions, guilty of illogic, painful to respecters of language. Wisdom poorly communicated lived by itself and died lonesome, a matter admitted. But where then to go? The Harvard catalogue didn't say.

Louis Lyons nodded. Yah, we were right. How about a seminar, a weekly seminar? Maybe Morrison would conduct it.

Morrison would. Without extra pay, at the cost of his own work as poet and novelist, without much recognition except from all nine of the ten of us who participated, he gave what he had to give. It was not insubstantial.

Bob Bordner, prime authority on the *Cleveland Press* snake, stopped me after one session. "You know, Bud," he said, "the words I've admired most in my writing have to be killed." He smiled under his longhorn mustache. "Too smart."

Without having seen his copy, I knew what he meant.

A handicap for beginners—perhaps the first trouble and certainly a particular trouble in efforts at fiction—is the felt requirement of an organized body of wisdom and the impressive display of it in a chunk or in chunks. Heaved into the flow of a story, the amateur thinks, it proves the right to write. What is proved is that the writer is an exhibitionist who needs a story doctor's advice to zip up. The egotism natural and maybe necessary to a writer, of which this prideful and bald demonstration is a prime symptom, must find its satisfaction in ways other than the localized proof that here is a man of parts.

A maxim follows. Whatever the wisdom of a writer, it does and must exist in dispersion, to be drawn on in fiction as fictional circumstances suggest, to be expressed bit by bit in the actions and reactions and thoughts and conversations of characters. To attempt an authorial concentration is not only to damn a story; it is to deform and disavow wisdom.

18

Long after my conversation with Bordner, Ted Morrison and I fiddled with a never-finished textbook for those who wished to write fiction. We started its sections with what we called maxims, the best of which were Ted's. I remember some of them and in practice recall and try to apply the whole lot. Listed then, with occasional illustrations, unranked in importance, are the ones that come to mind now.

Avoid when you can the pluperfect, alias the past perfect tense. By unexplained magic the past tense becomes present in reading. The pluperfect asks the reader to go backward in time to what is over and done with and hence less engaging than what happens now. The trick is not so difficult as you may imagine. Ordinarily one "had" is enough.

Example: He had rowed away from the island, leaving the boy. The boy stood at the edge of the water and shouted curses and gestured. "Come back, goddam you! Come back!" By and by distance stilled the voice and dusk enveloped the boy.

Seldom is the passive voice as good as the active. It slows the flow by asking the reader to relate the verb, not to a following object, but to a preceding subject. Here is a special point for reporters. Journalism too often demands that a key word be the beginner, as in: Resistance, even to the extreme of the hydrogen bomb, was promised if . . .

Remember how important is figurative language, imagery if you wish. A strong wind is not so strong as a wind like a hand in your face. In the area of imagery comes, too, the use of adjectives to modify nouns they don't really belong with. It used to be at hazing time that college sophomores tonsured the heads of freshmen. A journalism student wrote that one sophomore, having captured his man, plied the eager clippers. It was the sophomore who was eager, of course, but the transfer of the adjective made him all the eagerer. Finally, one sense can be employed to strengthen and enlarge the expression of another. Though it is poetry, E. A. Robinson's "The Dark Hills" is rich illustration.

> Dark hills at evening in the west,
> Where sunset hovers like a sound
> Of golden horns that sang to rest
> Old bones of warriors under ground . . .

Use with care loose descriptions, abstractions, words of large embrace. What does "beauty" mean or "beautiful" or "terrible" or "tragedy" or "ecstasy" or "magnificent"? Something, to be sure, and much sometimes. But illustrations and specifics are surer aids to ends.

Leave something to the reader. He has perception and imagination, more than you may think. Don't restrain him in your nest of adjectives and adverbs. Let him fly, remembering that nouns and verbs are the guts of language. Here's where the beginner goes astray. Having fallen short in the use of nouns and verbs, he tries to enforce his prose with adjectives and adverbs and, though he doesn't know it, thereby makes it weaker.

If you are inclined to leave your character solitary for any considerable length of time, better question yourself. Fiction is association, not withdrawal. It is love and hate and agreement and conflict and common adventure, not lonely musings on have-beens and might-have-beens. Mark as typical of the amateur the opening that finds Joe or Jim or Ethelbert waking up in a hotel room, alone and hung over. Where had he been? Who was that redhead who took him for drinks and dinner last night and then said she had to go home? At this point Joe sits up and runs his hands through his hair, which is seen by the author—who's lurking around somewhere—to be curly and tousled. Joe doesn't see it. He doesn't think about it. He has other things on his mind. That guy who bopped him? Damn him! What had it all been about? He wishes he could see through the mists. He wishes he had an eye-opener. Oh, God! Maude had been right when she said the big city wasn't for him. Maude was always right. Pretty, too.

We, the readers, are on Page Five now and will say goodbye. Goodbye and good riddance.

Your characters are yours to command, so command them. But exercise care. You can not make them be false to themselves. You can not show your power. Yet it is possible to bring a sudden end to a scene or to carry it on and enlarge it by manipulations of cast that arouse no suspicion. And it often sharpens a scene, though the scene be planted in the sensibilities of one character, to suggest his appearance and mood by means of a line or two of quotation from another. Suppose Joe is upset and frightened, it doesn't matter by what. Because he is your man, you may say—and very likely will—that he is upset and afraid and tries to hold his knees steady and forces a smile so as to cover his fright. Even were these lines put professionally, would they serve as well as an observation by another character? You might gain effect by having Jim say, "What's wrong with you, Joe? You look like you just seen a ghost."

Write a good scene and much else will be forgiven you. For convenience in teaching some teachers divide fiction into three parts—scene, summary or synoptic action and description. The terms mean what they suggest. Scene is action and dialogue. It is dramatization. It is theater. Summary bridges intervals in which nothing of much importance has happened. Description is description—of weather, geography, general or immediate setting. No matter the first importance of scene, it is well to remember that the three words are merely handles for analysts. If taken in practice as separate parts of a three-sectioned whole, they work ruin. So, another maxim:

The good writer does everything at once. This is a way of saying that good fiction avoids inertia. A passage devoted exclusively to description, with no relationship to the seer or even with a remote one, discourages readers. But how do everything at once? How put scene, summary and description together? A simple example: " 'We been ridin' this damn range for two months,' Bill said, yanking his saddle horse to a stop and squinting up at a sun that burned hot as a blister."

Not always do you have to write summary. Sometimes a white-space break serves as well or better.

A writer should keep asking himself: What am I doing to my reader? He may be doing what was never intended, with the consequence that he'll lose his reader through boredom or disappointment or both. He may fail to place the reader where the reader can perceive and participate. The reader, even though ignorant of the cause of dissatisfaction, needs to be rooted, needs to have a sure position if he is to enjoy a course of experience. Unsure, he's uncomfortable. Edith Merrilies, perhaps the greatest of classroom teachers, used to ask two questions not altogether irrelevant here. The questions were "Whose story is this?" and "What is this story about?" The writer had better be sure he knows and, more important, that the reader does, too. False leads, the arousal of expectations never fulfilled, are common with the amateur writer and disappointing to the reader. The man who said the end of a story should be implicit in the beginning must have been talking about false leads at least in part. What has been said in this paragraph and elsewhere bears on the first necessity: The reader must believe. "Plausibility," Miss Merrilies kept saying, "is the morality of fiction."

The bigger the theme, the less weight you need give it. If your story deals with the troubled subject of race, for instance, you may proceed in the knowledge that the problem already has been established in the minds of your readers, with the result that a touch will serve better than a blow.

Oftener than not restraint is superior to unbuttoned and pantyless revelation in matters of sex, even though there's no denying that naked cavortings, along with a superfluity of four-letter words, find ready readership. When I stumble onto a book that insists that I see all and hear all, I wonder if the author ever has heard or paid heed to an old Kentucky story: A sharecropper, shopping in town, went to a dry-goods counter for nightgown material for his wife. He found a cloth that pleased him immensely. "Good," the salesgirl said. "How much do you want?" He answered, "About forty yards." She told him, "My goodness! You don't need forty yards for one nightgown!" "I know," he explained. "But I get such a kick out of pullin' it up."

Be wary of the short short story. No longer so popular as it once was, it beckons beginners, perhaps because they equate brevity with short and easy going. Actually the form is difficult beyond their imagining. A related maxim:

There is no such thing—or there ought not to be—as a "surprise" ending. In the all-too-frequent manner of O. Henry it involves concealments from the reader, tortures of materials, tricks worked from left field. True surprise is recognition. It follows honestly from what has gone before. It makes the reader exclaim, "Why, sure! Why didn't I see that?"

One of the elements, or demands, of successful fiction is a continual, slight novelty. The maxim is a paraphrase of Edmond Gosse's observation and, hopefully—as word handlers say these days with high disregard of grammar—need not be extended.

Every word must bear its weight. Not for rhythm, not for roll, not out of love of your effusion, can you afford weak words. Which is not to say that you cannot manage rhythm and accent. It is to say that you must work, that you must discard much that you have liked and find through agony the necessary muscle. For want of a better place there may be included here the sometimes foolish and the usually superfluous words that beginning writers employ as adjuncts to dialogue. "She smiled, 'Where have you been?'" As if a smile enunciated. "He mused, 'What happens now?'" "'What?' he barked." "'Go to hell!' he said angrily." "'Goddammit!'

he cursed." The list is endless. These danglers—stretched figure, verb and adverb—are marks of the amateur.

What has been said by way of advice is advice and no more than that. The maxims are meant to be aids, not commandments. To one or all of them great exceptions exist—written by writers who knew what they were doing.

For what they're worth, a few tips apart from maxims:

Though heaven knows I've used many topic sentences in this chapter, I hope of necessity, I get more and more chary of them, especially in fiction. What profits a shotgun sentence like, "He could not believe what he saw"? Why not plunge in and show what the man saw? If it is extraordinary enough, the reader will recognize and share his astonishment.

In the laborious and lonely business of writing, how force, or cozen, yourself into facing the typewriter? Three recourses exist for me. If I have done a fair day's work and know what comes next, I knock off, assured that I can proceed in the morning. Under less happy circumstances I often gain some degree of momentum by retyping in the morning the final page I completed the night before. And sometimes I tell myself, "I'll work a half hour today and that's all." It seldom is all.

With notable exceptions college courses in creative writing are of little avail. Too often the teachers themselves are frustrated writers and hence at odds with the craft. Too often, absorbed in symbol, theme, mood and what not, they leave the student as lost as before. And sometimes, out of their own failures, they are sour at the prospect of student success. Where to go then? I vote for good writers' conferences, of which there are several.

: : : : : : :

19

: : : : : : :

The Nieman term neared its close, and we were sad. Soon now the splitting-up, the goodbyes to persons and places and a time already becoming a memory. Back to work, each of us, back to typewriters and makeup and headlines and clocks that seemed always to be pushing the deadlines. Never would any of us be the same as before. Would all of us ever meet in reunion?

As it was a time of approaching farewells, so was it a time for appraisal. What had we learned? In what new directions had our thinking been bent? What had we rejected and what embraced? Were we better men? Being better men, would we be better newspapermen?

I checked my acquisitions. I had added, it seemed enormously, to my scant knowledge of economics, government, international law, political science. Add American literature, for what I had known of it had been spotty. I knew more about history and had begun to understand what constituted good poetry. I had been confirmed in my convictions as to the responsibilities of a free press. I had learned much about the writing of prose. My increments, taken together, had extended my horizons and made me feel more at home even in a bloody world.

Prejudices? That first prejudice! A man tends toward the accepted positions of the society in which he moves. He may recognize their injustices. He may resist them. But race prejudice is a cancer in all stocks, white, black or brown, Christian or Jew, and needs constant watching and examination even by those who lay claim to immunity.

I knew from experience in Lexington that separate and equal education was separate but not equal and had said as much. I knew that the Negro enjoyed no equality before the law and I had spoken out. I doubted he ever would have equal opportunity, at least in my lifetime, and regretted that he wouldn't. I kept hearing, and kept denying, that Negroes were pushy and took separate seats in buses just so white people would have to sit with them. "Hell," I would answer. "If there's a vacant seat, I take it myself unless I spot a friend." Some people, advancing bits of evidence that I protested, called me a "nigger lover."

Then, one sleepy Saturday afternoon, I was waiting alone for a bus. As it pulled to a stop and I was about to step in, someone knocked me aside. I turned and saw a heavy colored woman where I had stood, and the unsuspected cancer broke open.

"Goddammit," I said, "you can get on first! You don't have to knock me down."

She cowered like a whipped dog. "Mistuh," she told me, panting, "I was waitin' a block up the street, and the white bus driver wouldn't stop for me, and I been doin' day work and got to get home to tend to my chirren. So I had to run."

I apologized, thinking about carcinogens.

Never again, I told myself after that Nieman term, would I be so susceptible. Never again would I settle almost comfortably in a tainted tradition and accept as much as I had. If not born equal, men were born with the right to an equal chance. I would fight for that kind of equality, for an equality that offered fair chance and equated equals with equals while recognizing the vast differences among men of whatever color.

Even as I summed up my acquisitions and sought to find positions through logic, a possibility stirred in my head. Maybe I wouldn't have to go home right away after all.

I talked to Louis Lyons again, this time on the Massachusetts Avenue curbing across from the subway burrow, a poor place for the request that beat in my throat. Louis didn't look at me. He looked in his crystal-ball smoke, unaware even of traffic.

An extension of my fellowship to mid-Agust? It was true, he answered, that extensions had been granted before, but only in a few special instances, compelling in nature. Yah. Very few.

"I could get time from my paper," I said, "and the extra weeks on my book—"

All at once I saw that the request was preposterous and, more than that, embarrassing to a friend. I could read "No" in the puffs of his pipe.

"Never mind, Louis," I told him. "I shouldn't have asked."

His long silence suggested agreement.

"I'll finish the manuscript anyhow."

"Yah," he said again.

"It was just that Ted Morrison said he was sure I would qualify for a fellowship at the Bread Loaf Writers' Conference the middle of August."

Abruptly he focused on me, and his pipe came out. "Ted Morrison?"

"Yes, but forget it." I didn't add that if I returned to Lexington at the end of the spring term I could not afford the transportation to and from Bread Loaf.

But again it was as if Louis didn't see me. Only his words acknowledged my presence. "Mind if I talk to Ted?"

The next day, I think it was, he gave yes to my application. Soon afterwards the family took off for a Montana summer, and I moved to a residence hall.

The two months I spent there were lonely. Family gone, Nieman friends gone, classrooms, professors, seminars gone. There remained, not for me to impose on overmuch, Ted Morrison, Louis Lyons, Benny DeVoto, Charlie Morton of the *Atlantic Monthly* and the few non-academic friends we had made. There remained the Widener Library and the typewriter with its demands on me.

In unproductive fits I read or reread *The Great Gatsby, The Charterhouse of Parma, Dracula* and other books that excused me from working on my own. I even had a go at *The Golden Bough* but could find no excuse there and said the hell with it. Reading, I wondered why so many people considered *Tender Is the Night* to be Fitzgerald's best work. I wondered about Charlie Morton's great liking for Stendhal.

But word by word and line by line my manuscript proceeded. Not in bursts, though. For me, writing is a slow and painful business. It demands concentration and search and presents the obstacles of dissatisfaction with what could be said better. And there's no immediate reward in putting words on paper. The reward, great but fugitive, is in having written, in having found the word, the line, the paragraph, the chapter that is as good as ever you can make it. I spent a full day on one line of dialogue and knocked off satisfied.

Lonely, I found company in my characters, who grew as I came to understand them. They assumed their own qualities independent of me and hence became more demanding. And names. They took or had taken their own with scarcely a thought on my part. Their independence, along with their development, made me almost superstitious. Writing ahead of my research, I kept finding my guesses jibed with the facts. A final experience came close to closing the case. One of my characters called himself Deakins, a name unheard of. A couple of years after I had completed my manuscript, I wandered along the crest of Independence Rock in eastern Wyoming. There, on what was called the great register of the desert, fur-hunters and others who followed the sun had painted or chiseled their names. One leaped to my incredulous eye. DEAKINS. Standing there, staring at a name inscribed long ago, gazing at distances too far for the mind to reach, I thought: I have been here before.

My manuscript was two-fifths finished when I set out for Bread Loaf. Looking back at my loneliness, renewing in recollection my almost physical hunger for the West, sometimes I think that whatever *The Big Sky* is, it owes much to nostalgia.

20

The Bread Loaf Writers' Conference, first and hence oldest and possibly still the best of short courses in writing, is a child of Middlebury College though removed from its mother by some thirteen miles. Planted on high ground near the mountain from which its name came, it consists physically of an inn, numerous cottages, a lecture hall, an old barn converted into a snack bar and dance hall, shade trees, clipped lawns and pruned shrubs, wild flowers past the reach of the lawnmowers and a wooded brook just a pleasant hike distant from its one gut of pavement. That was the count, anyway, when first and last I was there, and it was enough. Anything more would have seemed a trespass on completion.

The conference schedule offered an abundance of fare,

more indeed than one mind could take in—a fact recognized
by Ted Morrison, the long-time director, who advised Fellows and conferees not to tackle the full course but to pick
and choose according to interests. There were sessions devoted to the short story, the novel, the article, to biography
and poetry and drama. There were workshops and interviews
and night lectures and music recitals and, for the staff and
Fellows and special guests, convivial, late-hour discussions at
the faculty cottage. Days and nights offered their rich abun-
dances; and who would restrain his appetite though he
burst? Friendships developed by magic, and despite the
crowded program, groups and couples found time to sprawl
on the sun-warmed lawns or stroll under the trees in the soft
nights. No radios allowed and no TV sets. A place of seques-
tration, free from fret and formality, two weeks in a world
suspended above and independent of other planets. Walking
from cottage to classroom or down to the brook, seeing the
rise of the hills and the fairness of sky, I could imagine that
here was the West, here a private and precious preserve,
though I knew but a few of the plants, wild and tame, and
few of the fragrances.

The practice at meals, presumably aimed at the edifica-
tion of the cash customers, was to move us free-loading Fellows about in the dining room, to assign each of us one
table one day and another the next. So it came about that I
sat next to a woman of sixty-five years, maybe seventy. She
liked to write verse, she told me. Her manner suggested an
old and amused sophistication. She not only liked to write it,
she did write it. What was more, she sold it.

She must have read my doubt.

"Nothing to it," she said. "If I want to pick up five or
ten dollars, I write a godgimme. It's a sure thing."

I asked, "A godgimme?"

"Of course," she said with a lovely and incredible cynicism. "You know: 'God give me a garden with a hollyhock in it.' "

A small thing, cherished in memory, as small things so often are.

Then and later, as a teacher, I met people I shan't forget—Fletcher Pratt, Helen Everitt, Louis Untermeyer, Walter Havighurst, William Sloane, John Ciardi, William Hazlett Upson, Hervey Allen, Bruce Lancaster, Lovell Thompson, Edith Merrilies, Wallace Stegner, Robin White, Mary Moore Molony and so many others that a complete list would be hard to compile.

Bernard DeVoto was not a member of the staff the year that I was a Fellow, but he came for a visit. In preceding references I fear I've suggested I knew him better than I did. Except for a couple of casual encounters I hardly knew him at all at that time. A difficult man, a curmudgeon, given to extremes and tantrums, he made me uneasy, and uneasier still because he was an authority on the early West, a student with knowledge undoubtedly far beyond mine even in application to the limited years I'd researched. Fortunately, I didn't know that in a sense I had stolen his subject, and was writing the kind of novel he had long wanted to write and perhaps would have written already but for a growing shakiness of faith in himself as a writer of fiction.

He sat with a group of us on the porch of Cherry Cottage on the first day of his visit, and I thought, while he proclaimed the eternal truth on all manner of subjects, how ugly he was. He was a trifle under average height and had a bow in his upper spine, yet suggested animal power. Glasses dimmed but somehow exaggerated belligerent eyes set in a square face that could have been called hangdog save for his immense and articulate vitality. His mouth kept working under a nose that nature had shoved in, with the result that his nostrils were like those of a man seen supine.

After he had gone I said, "Without an umbrella he'd drown in the rain."

I shan't forget the rebuke. Robeson Bailey, then a professor of English at Smith, made an answer that mildness made stinging: "Here on the mountain," he said, "we don't talk of appearances."

In later years I came to admire DeVoto and we grew to be close friends. Outrageous he would always be and, often, difficult. He bristled when crossed. Carried away on the tide of an idea or an argument, he spouted extremes that reflection toned down and made plausible in his writing, vigorous and valorous though his writing was. As a teacher and speaker he was wont to bully students and audiences. He would have fought a bear.

But his behavior was all compensation, a bluff to conceal his compassion, a counter, one suspected, to an abiding uncertainty, to a self-diminishment that the man's self wouldn't let be diminished. Under that outward protection was another personality, a sturdy one to be sure, but one smiling and agreeable and generous, quick to help and to praise when praise was in order.

Another man might have resented my usurpation of his Western preserve, might have cried down through vexation the kind of a novel he'd had in mind before me. Not DeVoto. He read *The Big Sky* in manuscript and promptly beat all his drums to promote it.

Character, once it is known, alters countenances; and when I look back now I do not see the face on the porch of Cherry Cottage. I see Benny DeVoto, the whole man, and in glad company with the ancient dead whom we both know, we again sail together down the wide Missouri.

Over that first conference and the ones I attended thereafter there hovered the god, Robert Frost, who was not always the kindly old sage that English-department heads make him out to be but could be and often was the captive of fierce and aberrant passions—which may be a necessity to great poetry. Staff members with experience of him walked on tiptoe, wondering whether this or that would enrage or please Robert. One said, speaking of Robert's aversion to another poet of stature, that Robert was resolved to be the only bull in the pasture.

A full biography of Frost, yet to be written, must include his egregiousness. By well-founded hearsay, direct from witnesses or victims, I have perhaps a dozen reports of it, but because they are hearsay won't post them here. One example, mild by comparison, I can swear to, however:

We had arranged to have a baseball game, as was the annual custom. Captains had been appointed, sides chosen up. Frost and I were on opposite teams.

"Now, Bud," DeVoto advised me in advance of the contest, "you'd better let Robert's side win." I asked him why. He said, "If it doesn't, he'll chuck the conference."

I allowed for prejudice. It had been agreed once that DeVoto was to be Frost's official biographer. Not strangely, in view of their characters, the two had fallen out and there existed between them now, if not actual enmity, then something close to it.

On the field I began to believe DeVoto was right. Frost, though not young, was a pretty fair player, a point incidental to his complete and passionate involvement as a contestant. He argued about balls and strikes. He protested calls at the bases. Chin out, red-faced and furious, he kept confronting the umpire, waving wild arms as if ready to swing.

Watching, I wondered. Here on this otherwise peaceful afternoon, during an hour that was supposed to be fun, over a game the result of which could mean nothing, how could wisdom be so foolish? How could a man be so great and so small? Was hot concern over trifles an ingredient of greatness?

Frost's side won the game, and he came to the faculty cottage in high good humor.

I hadn't learned yet to separate a man from his works, to consider them independent one from the other and make judgments accordingly. It is easy to say but it takes effort to believe that if a work is great, then it is great, no matter what kind of person wrote it.

Not that Frost ever treated me badly. He was always friendly and kind, perhaps in the knowledge that I was no threat in his pasture. We had common interests in Montana, where his late daughter had lived and his son-in-law still resided. And we had a common fear of audiences, though I had not suspected that fear in Robert.

Yes, he said. Public appearances terrified him. Yet somehow they justified him as a man. The accident of time and circumstance had kept him from bearing arms for his country, and, while he was regretful, he was unsure that he would have had the courage that other men had. So public speaking was an alternate test of his courage. It was proof if not proof complete, and it helped reconcile him to himself.

A time or two, with the conference closed, I spent a few days with the Morrisons at their small farm just out of Bread Loaf and hardly a rifle shot away from Frost's summer home. We visited back and forth, and once I was astonished as well as delighted when, during a rainstorm, Frost showed up in a slicker, rain hat and gum boots.

Frost was a great conversationalist—which isn't to say

he was talky. His utterances tended to be cryptic and took strange and provocative turns. And he wouldn't speak about his own works, wouldn't say what he was trying to get at in a poem. He left interpretation to others.

Yet a stated conviction about all art at least threw light upon his own method. "Any piece of art," he told a group of us later, "must first of all tell a story." If something exists beneath, as it should, let people find it.

Frost talked about and was wont in his inquiring way to enlarge on little things. He was proud of his garden with its knotty carrots, tortured corn and barely surviving potatoes, all of them with flavors not found in the markets. Were they better, then, by having been grown in the bleak soil of Vermont? Did quality develop from hardship? He never quite asked the open question, yet the half-suggestion was there, and I bought it.

Once, when I trudged up to Robert's place—those who knew him always called him by his first name—I found him reviewing old papers. He had a letter or note in his hand. It had taken him far back to his hard days in England, before his voice sounded as a major American poet. He told me a little about that time. "My wife," he said with ancient appreciation, "my wife made time to sew."

He said a little more but need not have. There was such an old but present poignancy in the remark.

His wife, long dead, had found time to sew.

If Bread Loaf in my year as a Fellow in 1945 was free of frets, it was only for the first week. Then pressures began to mount, for soon if not right away Fellows and contributors would receive from staff members private, face-to-face appraisals of what they had written. A breeze of hysteria stirred and strengthened into a wind. Some would-be writers announced that they didn't care what was said, for their works were their own and to hell with criticism. They were the precious. Some were too meek. They were the eunuchs. Some knew, after attending the lectures and workshops, that their submissions needed revisions. They were the possibilities. Whatever the types, one and all ran a fever.

My summons came one waiting afternoon. Would I see Mr. Sloane at five o'clock?

Bill had my manuscript before him. He filled his pipe. That took some time. Once he had lighted his fire, he raised his hazel-nut, hypnotic eyes. He asked, "How near are you through?"

I said, "Two-fifths, maybe."

And how long would it take me to finish?

I said that depended. I had to go back to my job.

He puffed on his pipe and shook his head in what seemed like negation. "This is great stuff," he told me, "simply great."

I panted my thanks.

Would I consider, he asked, a five-thousand-dollar advance?

It was hard to consider. I had never seen that much money all in one pile.

The trees weren't there, or cottages, or friends, as I raced to Bread Loaf's single phone. From it I wired Harriet: "Swinging on a star. Five thousand in advance."

I think I knew then that I was done, or close to done, with newspapermaking.

I had to return to *The Leader*, though it had never
paid its news staff enough. Few newspapers do. But in its pa-
ternalistic way it had been generous, generous beyond the
limits of some liberal papers I know, or did know. It had
paid me in full during the months of my illness. It had seen
me through times of other distress. It had given me four-
week vacations. It had backed me at the bank and made my
house possible. It had given me almost a year off, yet held my
place open. More than that, it had supplemented my stipend
at Harvard. Without its unsought checks, I doubt that I
could have managed. So I had to go back and to go back
with thanks.

The institution, the establishment—not *The Leader*

except as a small part of it—is the target of my pot shots at journalism. I look back with a sense of indebtedness not unmixed with complaint on my years in the newsroom. Sometimes I ask how many years were misspent. Oftener I find pleasure in the view, in the recalling of old incidents, the redoing of old deeds, the refreshment of faded pride, the renewal of friendship. Good men grew up under me or despite me, and I matured under them. Four of us won Nieman Fellowships. No paper of even roughly comparable size had such a record. Perhaps none has yet.

On my return the boss told me to manage my time as I chose, to make room in my schedule for work on my manuscript. I name him tardily: Fred B. Wachs, eventually general manager of both *The Leader* and *Herald*. Put in an hour or two hours or half a day in the newsroom, he said, long enough but just long enough for needed direction. Then go home and tackle my typewriter. I'd get my salary.

I quit nonetheless, but not before months had gone by and not before I could believe I had discharged my obligation in full. I had worked there for twenty-one years.

When someone asks, as someone inevitably does, whether I don't miss the smell of printer's ink, I answer no. I am glad to have escaped the disciplined madhouse of the newsroom, glad to have found more fulfilling and freer employment, glad to have made and to be making more money. If regrets remain, one is the loss of that community intimacy that is a newpaperman's special possession, that knowledge of subjects and men and associations and stresses that lie underneath news. Maybe I would like to edit a paper if free of checkreins. I suspect there's that much of the messiah in me. And, call it habit or a recognition of values, I still read the papers I get—spot news, editorials, columns, sports, even the stock-market reports.

I do not know how the journalism graduate enters the newsroom these days. We did so on tiptoe, thinking back to the recent madcap careers that gave the business a touch not found any more. If he does enter, I wonder if he's more concerned with overtime than well-done. He may not enter at all, having chosen radio or TV or any of other numerous specialties listed in a generous curriculum. Journalism schools, like all bureaucracies, are pregnancy-prone and have birthed families, in part legitimate, that the high courts have surnamed Communications.

The schools, I'm sure, have raised newspaper standards, yet the degree is impossible to establish. Only a few dailies, a comparative few, are first-rate. At work against excellence is economics. The large and hopeful, free and incorruptible policy, though it does come sometimes, doesn't come easily to an endeavor that has grown to involve hundreds of thousands or millions of dollars. That kind of money rules in favor of compromise and restraint. The corruption of possession enters the operation and, inevitably, the blight of the corporate mind. Pushed to his last line of defense, the corporate or individual operator may say, as he has said, "Look! I run this paper. I damn well can do what I want to do with it." It is here that freedom of the press becomes the freedom not to be free.

These observations don't imply a defiant dishonesty. They point to an understandable, if regrettable, caution, restriction and appeasement through silence, all of which the publisher can defend, to himself anyway. He is afraid, though he dislikes to admit it, of great areas of human interest and hot conflict. He doesn't want controversy or canceled subscriptions.

It would be unfair not to acknowledge the improvement that has come about in two or three decades. Words and subjects once taboo are now common. We read much of birth control, not so long ago avoided or treated sketchily because it meant the sure arrival of virulent committees. When cigarettes were first suspect as cancer causes, too many papers spiked that news in deference to advertisers. Now we're kept informed. Honest words like "abortion," "rape" and "pregnant" once kept us deskmen busy seeking substitutes. I suppose "piles" would pass now, too, though in older days on my paper it was a word all right in advertisements but offensive next door in the news columns.

Allow the progress then, with thanks, but don't go overboard.

Good magazines tend to be freer, yet they too have their fears. I would count it forlorn to submit to any of them an article about the prevalence of perverts at Y.M.C.A.'s.

But book-publishing! Have something to say and say it well enough, and it will appear between covers, let the toes hurt that it tramps on. Here, with book publishers, stands the great redoubt of freedom of the press.

The quality that editorial fondness calls objectivity doesn't quite go over with me, either as reader or writer. It is impossible of attainment; even the choice of an opening sentence in a news story is a subjective decision. Not that I argue at all for the slanted story but that the vaunted objectivity is flat, that it has not the dimensions that promote understanding. A reading of Page One leaves the reader blind with the dust of events, unable to see clearly where the dust comes from. The reader needs interpretation as informed and as honest as informed and honest minds can make it. The current solution to the problem—and I fear it is the only one—is the editorial page and the syndicated column. The good papers make an honest and often successful attempt to provide what the news stories don't or can't.

Yet the gospel that the reporter has no opinions troubles me as it always has.

In place after place the working newsman performs at a peril that is half his creation. In the popular image he is a cynic; yet if old observations are valid, he is the opposite. His cynicism is merely a cloak for ideals. He wants to believe he's worthwhile in his niche and that the sum of the niches is wise and unselfish service. It is as if, through self and association, he must justify his habitation of earth. He lives in the hope that he and his colleagues are making his paper the good and effective social influence that a good publication should be.

Now suppose he meets restraints, denials, positions he cannot in conscience support, as he will and in many cases should, since inexperience however lofty makes a poor pilot. No matter. He meets enough wrong resistances, enough dubious pressures. He protests and yields and protests and yields, and slowly his will atrophies. He may retreat then into the celebrated cynicism of the craft. It is far more likely, though, that he will let his wish for virtue seduce him. He will rationalize. His paper does some good. Why, it does a *lot* of good. The positions of the publisher come to have merit. By this manner of thinking, by this diminishing adjustment, he justifies himself.

Corruption out of idealism by surrender!

In 1946 *The Big Sky* got itself completed, or it got me to complete it. Hours and weeks and months of slave labor went into it. Working, I could look back on what I had done with some satisfaction, but what remained to be done appalled me. Part of the reason was that I had made no chapter-by-chapter or scene-by-scene outline. I thought then, as I think now, that I would be imprisoned by such a projection. I had a theme, not original, that each man kills the thing he loves. If it had any originality at all, it was only that a band of men, the fur-hunters, killed the life they loved and killed it with a thoughtless prodigality perhaps unmatched. Yet in the absence of an outline the typewriter was errant or balky. It produced pages of junk or no pages at all. I cursed it day after day.

But the end came. Clutching the manuscript, knowing only that I couldn't do better, I set out for New York, so exhausted as to be numb to all consequences. Even the welcome it and I got left me indifferent if not unappreciative. A thing done was done, and already my mind had fixed itself on the Oregon Trail and a new book, *The Way West*.

I wasn't prepared for the praise the published book got. Me, an important new author? Me, a fresh voice out of the West? Me? I read the reviews and looked at the pictures and, though pleased, felt somehow diminished while my family rejoiced. Though my being had gone into it, the book wasn't mine now, and what comments were made about it were like voices heard in the distance. Here I was, apart from it, and tomorrow I would fall on my face.

Once *The Big Sky* caught on, there followed a flock of invitations to cocktail parties, luncheons, public appearances, interviews and afternoons for autographs. For the sake of sales, out of excitement and considerations of courtesy, I tried to oblige, and think now I shouldn't have. I was out of character. I belonged with my partner and enemy, the typewriter.

The University of Montana, my alma mater, wrote to ask if I would appear on the campus and accept an honorary doctorate of letters and, incidentally, make a short speech. Such men as John Mason Brown and Clarence Streit, the letter set forth, had appeared for doctorates before me. Of course I replied yes. So there came the ceremony, the investiture, the speech. If I have the order of procedure wrong, it is because I was terrified.

A day or two later my old friend, the fine craftsman Joseph Kinsey Howard, then teaching at Montana, told me in high glee that I'd received the wrong honor. I was to have been made a Doctor of Letters. Somewhere in the works the instructions got fouled, with the result that the parchment and cape signified a Doctor of Literature, a pitch above that of mere Letters. Just before the ceremony someone discovered the error. The committee or faculty—whoever was in charge of such things—met in hasty and high consternation. But the cape had been made and the sheepskin prepared. What the hell.

My degree has been framed, and, when occasion offers, I wear my cape proudly, for I am unique: the one and only Doctor of Literature by inadvertence.

The Big Sky gave me a financial footing. *Holiday* magazine, with as expert an editorial staff as I have ever encountered, helped out with a couple of assignments, one for a piece about Montana, the second about Kentucky. It was in doing these articles that I discovered how much more demanding is the journalism of magazines than the journalism of newspapers. The comparison is not odious: magazines aren't in a daily race with the clock.

While I prospered, my publishers were going broke, not because they weren't good publishers but because they had begun business just prior to a slump and had no backlist—like, say, a cookbook—to sustain them.

Under their pressure, in six months of such effort as I'll never be able to muster again, I wrote *The Way West*.

In it, for the first time, I had to get into the minds of women. I shrank. How understand women when they didn't seem to understand themselves? I found though, I hope, that the buds of the opposite sex that abide in us all can be awakened, can be brought at least to some bloom if imagination works hard enough. I wanted a preacher in the book, too, and here an old stroke of luck struck again.

Years before, in lean days, I had paid ten cents for a pamphlet that a Hoosier minister had written about his experiences on the Oregon Trail in 1841–42. A poor thing of forty-odd pages, cheaply bound, devoted to righteous fulminations, the pamphlet gathered dust for two or three years. Joseph Williams' one admirable trait was his courage. Penniless, at the age of sixty-four he had traveled a course that few men but rough trappers and traders had traversed before him. He never complained unless there be classified as complaint his fierce grief about sinning companions, on whom he called down heaven's mercy and wrath. He was never in fear. God was with him.

In a casual conversation with a rare-book dealer from Crawfordsville, Indiana, I learned that the pamphlet might have some value, maybe considerable. At home next day I found it in a clutter of papers and took it downtown for him to see. Yes, he said, it was the one, and it was worth a good deal, he didn't know how much. Neither was he much interested in buying it since it was outside his own field. But I'd better inquire.

So I did. The Huntington Memorial Library in California, without suggesting a price tag, promptly replied that I had the third copy known to be extant.

I sent letters to the dealers I knew of. Within a couple of days there came telegrams and long-distance calls. And I had mislaid the pamphlet at the hotel where I had talked to my friend! I scrambled downtown and was lucky enough to retrieve it.

The first offer came at night from Goodspeed's in Boston. Would I settle for $300? I would not. I said I had other letters of inquiry out. The offer doubled, then tripled. I made a pretense of indifference, as if I had more than fifty dollars in the bank and no unpaid bills. In the parlor, listening, my wife and a friend from the United Press wrung their hands. I had hardly cradled the phone than it rang again. Eberstadt & Sons in New York was ready with $1200. Shakily I gave a firm no.

In that hectic night I sold the flimsy piece for $1525. Later I found out I could have got more. Even so, I had made a solid ten-cent investment, though it was reduced by the thirty dollars I had to pay for a reprint.

Here, then, when I began to think about *The Way West*, was my preacher. Here he was, with his narrow morality and his conviction that a personal god kept score on curses, carnality and skepticism. I would make fun of him.

I didn't, though. I couldn't. He grew away from me. Brother Weatherby, as I named him, came to command my admiration, regardless of our differences. By God, if I could say so in his presence, he was a man. He taught me that serious fiction doesn't lampoon.

Some weeks after the manuscript had been completed, we set out again for Montana and the university's short course in writing at Missoula, where I was to teach. We made the trip with no decline of old elation and at Missoula fell in with established friends, among whom was Joe Howard, the director. Came a lull in the conference, and Joe and I went downtown. A telegram awaited me at the hotel. I opened and read it and, unbelieving, passed it slowly to Joe. It said I had made the Book-of-the-Month Club. Joe let out a whoop.

He couldn't wait to get back to the campus and announce the glad news. You would have thought my good fortune was his. He was that way.

Now I was in the real money, or thought I was, not having learned yet that the Federal government and the Internal Revenue Service held to the tradition that the place for authors was attics. Federal administrations kiss art in swift passing and hurry on, money in hand, for assignations with oil wells, office buildings and the dear fruits of the soil.

Months more or less idle passed after our return to Kentucky. I was lazy or exhausted, one or both; and it began to seem foolish, once I'd been introduced to the ways of tax-gatherers, to make any more immediate money. However, I did take an assignment from *Holiday*. Working on it, I found I needed some data that my old friends in the newsroom could look up.

I called. One of the friends said, "Congratulations, Bud."

I asked for what.

"You've won the Pulitzer Prize. Just came in on the wire."

Forty-five minutes later, I found I had won it. A telegram to that effect came from Dwight D. Eisenhower, then president of Columbia University.

Those years were memorable and made the more memorable by a trip I took with Benny DeVoto down the Missouri River, from headwaters to confluence.

Bill Lederer, not yet *The Ugly American* or the herder of *A Nation of Sheep,* arranged for the Missouri River junket in 1950. We had met him at Bread Loaf and seen him since, and we liked him. Although he had had numerous pieces published, he appeared to think that an outing with us would give him the real secret of authorship. He was a commander in the Navy then, at work in the Pentagon and, to get military approval, must have exercised his genial powers of persuasion, which a tendency to stammer only enhanced. The Air Force would fly us, he wrote, from Washington, D.C., to Great Falls, Montana, where the Corps of Engineers would take us in hand.

Neither Benny nor I had promoted the program, and

neither of us much liked our position, not wanting to be either ingrates or captives or, least of all, questionable beneficiaries of governmental largess. The prospect must have disquieted Benny more than it did me, for I entered on the excursion with no predetermined opinions other than an unstudied respect for the Corps. But Benny had been critical and outspoken. He had said multi-purpose dams existed only in bureaucratic imagination, for no dam could fulfill satisfactorily the four functions of flood control, navigation, irrigation and power. He had said that when the Corps of Engineers and the Bureau of Reclamation combined forces, as they had on the Missouri, even the Chief Executive was powerless.

With Lederer's help we rationalized. The airmen had to get in their time anyway; the Missouri trip would be taken with or without us; what mattered a couple of guests?

We gathered in Washington and found that a young and personable Army officer would accompany the three of us. We would take off two days hence.

That day was raw and windy. With an offhand competence that I envied, the two young airmen nosed the craft into the gusts and got her aloft. The plane was a converted B-25. Only later, praise be, was I told, right or wrong, that the model was treacherous.

One of the men came back from the cockpit and showed us how to harness up our parachutes, just in case. Benny grinned, and I grinned. We'd never get hooked up in time. Benny said, "Keep 'er flying."

We did keep flying but not where we wanted. We had pointed for Omaha as the first stop, but the pilots got word that the wind was so fierce there that all planes were grounded. One of them came back and reported as much. He was disgusted. You would have thought a surrender to wind was pure weakness. So, on a journey that was to have taken us quickly over a large section of the Oregon Trail, on over South Pass and northwards to the Upper Missouri, we wound up in Chicago.

We got out two days later. Now, in her whimsey, spring had turned mild. Below us was the new green of fields and woods, unstirred by wind, soft in the sunshine. Almost before we knew it, we were over the Oregon Trail, looking down, Benny and I, on landmarks we had looked up to before, traveling in minutes, traveling in one short afternoon distances translated into so many days and so many weeks and so many months by long-dead Oregoners whose vanished ox trains labored below us and were gone with the turn of a prop.

Benny showed a quiet excitement. It was almost as if he were on the way home, though he had renounced the West years before and gone to the Eastern Shore. Yet he kept writing about the Rocky Mountain region, and he kept coming back. I said to him once, after he'd stated anyone was a fool to live in the West, "Benny, you remind me of a man who has left his wife only to find that if he couldn't get along with her, neither can he get along without her."

His small smile was agreement.

At our altitude Courthouse and Chimney Rocks were minute but distinct. They skimmed beneath us. Rushing toward us were Scott's Bluff, Independence Rock, the Sweetwater, Devil's Gate, the entrance to South Pass between the Wind and Rattlesnake ranges.

Mountain men, home-seekers, small- and great-souled missionaries alike misled by the mirage that had the red men loving Jesus instanter—these we knew. Ours was a time of reunion with all of them, though it was made upstart and insulting to their ancient labors by the speed of our passing.

Down there were Ashley and Fontanelle, Tom Fitzpatrick, Jim Bridger and the men of the fur brigades. Down there were Marcus Whitman and Narcissa, Father Pierre Jean DeSmet and others who thought to bring the Big Medicine of the Bible to people barely out of the Stone Age. Down there were Brigham Young and Parley Pratt and the Saints who would establish the most successful theocracy on record. Down there were the home-seekers like those under Elijah White, like Joel Palmer, from whose journal I'd borrowed. There were others, friends of Benny's, whom I had met only in passing. In *Across the Wide Missouri*—Benny's best book, to my mind—he had come to know more of them than I, and to know them more intimately. We waved and flew on, reluctant and guilty.

We tilted around and came back over South Pass, wanting to see it as had men who backtracked to report in the East on the fortunes of God and of beaver. We turned north then, over the Bighorns, over the blue Absarokas, and let down at Great Falls, where Joe Howard met us.

We had quite a welcome that night. In addition to Joe, whom we liked and respected, the party included Norman Fox, a good writer of good westerns, who was even a better man than he was a writer; Mildred Walker, the novelist, and her husband, Dr. Ferd Schemm, both of whom had wide and duly earned reputations; old friends of one or more of us all, including George Jackson, my boyhood companion, who locked up his barbershop and drove from Choteau down to Great Falls. Benny contended that Dempsey's Inn on the outskirts of town was the only place in the West that knew how to concoct a decent martini. I'm in no position to say he was wrong.

The men of the Air Force departed next morning, leaving us in the hands of the Corps of Engineers, who had flown to Great Falls the personal plane of General Lewis A. Pick, then ranking officer of the Corps. It was his name, along with that of William Glen Sloan, of the Bureau of Reclamation, that went to designate the program for the development of the Missouri as the Pick-Sloan plan. The two agencies, once in disagreement on the subject, found their differences readily resolved after U.S. Senator James E. Murray of Montana had proposed the establishment of a Missouri Valley Authority more or less along the lines of the Tennessee Valley Authority.

We flew to the headwaters of the Missouri, to the Three Forks, that once-savage heartland of the Blackfeet Indians where more than one seeker of beaver had lost his scalp. Turning downstream, we passed over the Great Falls of the Missouri, which the Montana Power Company had destroyed with a dam, over sleepy Fort Benton, less than a century earlier the bustling terminus of river navigation, over the site of old Fort MacKenzie, whose abandoned properties the Indians had burned, over the mouth of the Marias River, which the men of the Lewis and Clark expedition, against the prevailing hunch of their leaders, insisted was the Missouri and the real Missouri its tributary.

Known places again. Known stories. Old history come alive. Past into present. The forgotten remembered. It was in bemusement that we dropped down to Fort Peck, there to enter the actual, only half-welcome present.

General Pick was there to greet us, as were General Robert W. Brown and others high in the hierarchy. Then or later we met most men of rank, including General Samuel D. Sturgis, who was to become head of the Corps, and Reclamation's Mr. Sloan.

Our hosts were disarming. Gentlemen to a man, they entertained questions with patience. They endured dissent without anger. They saw to our physical comfort and complied with every request. No one could find fault with their hospitality.

In the realm of ideas though?

I see Benny looking small but looming large there with the brass. General Pick, with an air almost mystical, supports the Corps and the Plan. He talks of the needs of generations unborn. He sees industries where industries have never been and to our minds never can be. He speaks of war and the military advantage of a developed Missouri. And Benny stands up to him and asks how many transcontinental railway lines, easily reparable if bombed, could be built with the money that is going into vulnerable dams. The question goes unresolved.

The Corps doesn't promote itself, say its spokesmen. It doesn't encourage projects. It merely answers public demand. And Benny, restraining himself, replies with a euphemism for nonsense. He knows better.

It was in their great and narrow dedication that the Engineers provoked us. It was in their bureaucratic caste. I suggested to one of them that reforestation and the restoration of grasslands might be a better means of flood control than dams. "Maybe so," he answered, "but that's not our job. Our job is to build dams."

What about silt on this highly silty river? How long before the reservoirs filled up and dredges had to be employed? No problem there, I was told almost airily. First there was the dead water, deep and unmoving in the reservoirs. What did it matter if it was replaced by silt? I suspected some illogic here, but my man went on. Studies proved, he assured me, that silt would pose no difficulty for —I believe he said—something like one hundred and sixty-four years. That time seemed short to me, short for poster-

ity, short for the substitution for a river of a shallow, soupy
sea. More, having seen many reservoirs fill up quickly, I was
doubtful of his figure.

We asked the Engineers if we could borrow a small
boat, one, say, sufficient for the four of us, for we wanted the
experience of traveling at least a portion of the river in a
manner approximating that of travelers long before our
time. They looked at Benny and me as if wondering how mad
writers could be, but shortly came up with a craft that was
used to take soundings and so had a well in its middle. It
accommodated not only the four of us but a likable civilian
employee who attended to the outboard motor. We pushed
off just below Fort Peck Dam.

It was early spring, there in the high north, and the
mallards were pairing off, and the great gray geese; and the
red and diamond willows, not yet in leaf, showed the reviving
shades of salmon and tan and gold. To look at them was to
look at the hues of sunrise. And at sunset in the lengthening
days before solstice, the whole West promised salvation.
There, there behind us, was the glory, the final, seductive,
elusive beatitude that generations of men had pursued.

On the bosom of the Missouri, with only the impertinent
motor to deny us identity, we were the early explorers. No
fences came to view, no cultivated fields, and if occasionally
we saw a solitary cow, it was a buffalo. Only old things in
sight—the wood cuttings of beaver, the bark of cottonwoods
gashed high by vanished ice, the white pelicans of ancient
record aloft with heads like hatchets, a beaver on the shore
and then in the stream, his tail spanking water with a clap as
startling as a pistol shot. Then he would be gone, leaving for
a moment the rippled history of his going. And of a sudden a
great willow-fretted sandbar yielded to the river and fell
churning close to us, and the Missouri took over its tenancy.

Just as of old. Just as if the old were now. And Benny and I were Lewis and Clark, seeing as they saw, running aground as they did, getting sunburned and calloused and developing that look of wonder that stares at you from old reports. We looked at each other. He called me Deacon, either because of my heritage, long since renounced, or my appearance. I called him Pope or Brigham Young, for he was born half Mormon and half Catholic. But we were Lewis and Clark. Or we were Maximilian or Bradbury or Brackenridge or any of those bygone venturers who had converted us.

The Army Engineers kept careful watch. Three times a day they sent the DC-3 over to make sure we hadn't fallen victim to wind or ripple or the varmints of the wild. The plane would dip its wings, and we would wave, amused, and the plane would fly back to report that all was well with literature. Indeed it was. The one thing we missed was Sacajawea, whom the Engineers could hardly be expected to provide.

We drifted on. We knew where we were, in a sense, in the old sense, but had little idea of our position with reference to the upstart towns that had dared to assert themselves during the century and more we had so happily erased.

Like proof of our antiquity, a little boy appeared. He sat on a high bank, fishing all alone, his eye fixed on the red bobber below him.

We pulled closer, and Benny yelled, "Say, son, can you tell us where we are?"

To the author of *Across the Wide Missouri* the boy yelled back, "Mister, you're on the Missouri River."

Not only did the Engineers scout us by plane; they sent along a land party whose members picked us up in midafternoon or later, according to the dictates of offshore accommodations, and drove us to food and lodging in some small town or other beyond sight of the river. We knew when we were near a town, though we might not know the name of it. Sparkling when the sun was right, dazzling at a distance, lovely with refractions on tin cans—the town dumps on the bank told us.

One day it rained and rained and kept on raining, and the land crew lost its way. We put to shore against a hillside and considered. Night was drawing on. Our Engineers' civilian said we'd best hoof it up the hill. Up there somewhere there was our road. Maybe we could hitch a ride to town. He guessed it was five miles away.

The hill, we found, was solid gumbo, that white clay which, when wet, unites with leather and multiplies itself with every step. So we hardly hoofed it. We slipped and struggled and stomped and laughed and cursed and arrived breathless at the crest, each with pounds of gumbo on each shoe.

Nor was the road any better. It was gumbo, too. We stood forlorn, anchored to the earth, and in the dark and rain and distance waited for a miracle.

It came in the form of a small old car and a driver who identified himself as a Seventh-Day Adventist missionary among the Assiniboines. He told us to get in. He was bound for town.

We were reluctant, for his car was clean, and asked him to wait until we'd scraped our mud off. We found some twigs and a few splinters of old board and set to work. No use. We'd remove the pancake plasters from one shoe and set it down and scrape the second, only to find that the first one had gathered as much gumbo as before.

"Benny," I said finally, "I wish I was the strongest man in Ireland."

He hadn't heard that ancient story.

I told him, "The strongest man in Ireland could stick his thumb in his ass and hold himself out at arm's length."

Benny laughed harder than I ever heard him, and we piled in, gumbo and all, and went to town.

When we got there, Benny and I pressed some money on the missionary. He was a good man, so good, I fear, that instead of spending it to get his car cleaned up, he gave it to the cause.

Benny was so many things. Right or wrong, he had ideas on every subject I could mention. We got onto the matter of perversion and the repugnance it arouses in true males.

As I recall, he said, "It offends us beneath our efforts to understand or to condone because it is a denial of the biological purpose of intercourse—which is procreation."

"What about contraception, then?"

His answer, again in my remembrance, was that birth-controllers at least went through the right motions with the right sexes.

And how come, I asked him once, this not-infrequent switch of true believers, like the Catholics and the Communists.

A search for the godhead, he answered. For survival some people had to latch onto the presumed truth, the presumed leader, the godhead. Both sides, being absolute, had their private own.

Benny was fun. We got tipsy once and danced to the music of a juke box at some forgotten settlement and got up feeling sheepish; and I liked him better, this man of mind, for his frivolity.

In a larger boat, a steamer, we passed the entrance of the Platte. Next day, obligingly, our hosts churned the ves-

sel back upstream, as Bill Lederer had wanted them to.
When we reached the Platte again, Benny and I heaved Bill
overboard as old keelboatmen and steamboatmen and other
initiates, bound for outposts, used to do with greenhorns—a
practice presumably derived from sailors' antics when cross-
ing the equator. The crew retrieved Bill, and we received
him as a mountain man. This bit of foolishness delighted
Benny.

A good companion, Benny, and far more than that.
Whatever his tantrums, whatever his oddities, here was a
man fierce for the right.

By plane and flatboat, by plane again and car and
launch and steamboat, we reached St. Louis, that one-time
gateway to the West, passing fabled rivers on the way whose
convergences were drowned or would be drowned by dams.

In advance of destination, where we broke up with regret, we spent some time at Kansas City. Here was the show-
piece, the ultimate of engineering, and we must see how science had improved the lot of man. We gazed on the Kaw or
Kansas River, high-shored with concrete. We toured the
banks of the Missouri and saw the miles of piling. We looked
on acres of reclaimed land, where new factories gleamed.

We were told on the highest authority that in this fash-
ion all rivers should be harnessed. Never again—the predic-
tion was unanimous—would Kansas City suffer a major
flood.

I dislike to report, because I liked our hosts, that the
very next year the worst flood in its history visited the city.

23

In 1951 I went to Hollywood, there to write a screen-play based on a thin western novel called *Shane*.

I had never considered Hollywood or imagined I would be summoned. I had never written a screenplay. I had never even seen one on paper. When my agency called, I was in-credulous. Yes, the agency assured me, George Stevens at Paramount was to be the producer-director, and he was an uncommon man, one that I'd enjoy working with. I had never heard of him. I said I wanted to read the book.

Although Jack Schaefer, the author, betrayed some ig-norance about the West that I knew—he came to know a lot more—his prose had drive, and it introduced into the myth of the West a couple of elements which, if not unique, were fresh and engaging nevertheless. One was that the story came from the observations and through the senses of a small boy. The other was that a triangle was kept innocent by the admiration of each character for the others. You would hardly have thought that situation had much appeal to the industry.

I asked how it had happened that Hollywood's lightning had struck me. Because, said the agency, Stevens had asked Howard Hawks, the well-known director, whether he knew someone who could write effective western dialogue. Hawks, together with Ed Lasker, had just bought the screen rights to *The Big Sky.* He had recommended me.

Misgivings drove me to accept the assignment, though the salary of $1500 a week was no deterrent.

Stevens and I had lunch on the day of my arrival. He was both friendly and thoughtful, a heavy-set man with the look of resolve, and I liked him at once and gained a bit of assurance. He wanted to know what ideas I had. I confessed my ignorance of the mechanics of script writing but went on to say that I had always wondered at the absence of grief in western pictures. Here would be bodies strewn all around, but where were the funerals and where the mourners? Corpses had to be disposed of, and everyone had kinsmen or friends. Stevens seized on the suggestion. I remember saying, too, that there was no complete right or complete wrong in the stands taken by open-range ranchers and homesteaders. Each side had its case. Again Stevens agreed. What else was said as to story I cannot recall, except that in the main we accepted the Western myth, as we had to if we were to stay with the book.

I spent the first week reading sample scripts, though it seemed rather ridiculous for the studio to be paying for my education. Then, haltingly, I went to work, often consulting with Ivan Moffat, Stevens' associate. The two, it became clear, had had frequent discussions.

Even so, as the weeks went on I felt the need of talking to Stevens. My first draft was done, and I was eager for him to see it and give me the benefit of his judgment. But Stevens was busy launching *A Place in the Sun*, that adaptation of *An American Tragedy*, and couldn't be reached. I fiddled around. I felt guilty about drawing my pay. It was then that Joe Sistrom, another producer at Paramount and a man with an exceptional mind and a fondness for mathematics, introduced me to the theory of the third digit. Don't worry, he said. In any sequence the third digit, reading left to right, had little significance. If a picture was budgeted at $1,000,000, what mattered it if the third figure, naught, became a one and so made the total $1,010,000? Chickenfeed in the big money. Thereupon I felt less restive and would have felt underpaid had I known how much money *Shane* was to make.

Later, with our friendship established, Sistrom and I got to talking about coincidence, that bane of editors and picture-makers alike. Truth is so much stranger than fiction that when fiction employs truth's coincidences, it seems convenient, manufactured and false. But not quite, Joe said. If coincidence works to the advantage of a villain, if the villain in a fight spots and employs a chance weapon, then the public will believe, whereas it wouldn't were the case reversed. That thought was new to me, but it was and is true, and I wonder why. Do people want right beleaguered? Would they arm wrong? Out of experience do they suspect it is in the nature of things that right, if it is to prevail, must survive handicaps? Is coincidence the devil's due?

Not for more than a year did I see *Shane*. It had been kept in the can, as they say, until *High Noon* passed into sunset, a matter of timing. When I did see it, I sat stunned and incredulous. I hardly recognized my own stuff. It was, if not the best, then high among the best of all the westerns I had ever seen. My conviction was supported by the reviews it received, by the gate it drew and by its inclusion in five nominations for the Academy Award, which I think it deserved. I speak with modesty, for it was the genius of Stevens that made the film what it was. Under a grade-B director it would have been a grade-B picture.

Since then I have returned to Hollywood several times. I wrote the play eventually called *The Kentuckian*, taken from a book titled *The Gabriel Horn*. It turned out perhaps a little better than fair. If the result wasn't what I had hoped for, again I had worked with people it was a pleasure to work with, notably in the persons of Jim Hill and Burt Lancaster of the then firm of Hecht-Hill-Lancaster. Later, for Columbia, I did a treatment of David Lavender's fine book, *Bent's Fort*, not yet produced.

And I undertook one forlorn project. Friends ask me why the writers of novels don't rewrite them as screenplays. It's silly for studios to engage somebody else. I tended to think so myself. I learned better when I came to California to make a screenplay of my book, *These Thousand Hills*.

I was too close to my novel, too committed to words and pages and characters and the turns of the story to use a knife, to divide and discard and reassemble and reduce to the size of a short story a full-length book, as moviemakers must do. A book may require a day, even more, to read through. Who will spend that much time in a theater? People compare books and films, usually to the discredit of the latter, without understanding necessities. The necessity was too much for me when I tried to shrink my book to the dimensions of a play. Though, after it had been doctored to order by a studio writer under long-term contract, the film version lost the values I had struggled for in my novel, I'm still firm in the belief that a novelist ought to leave his novel alone. Other writers without blood ties to it can do better.

Of the problems confronting Hollywood perhaps the greatest is the disparity in the tastes of moviegoers. Young people compose the mass gate, and too often adult pictures don't attract teen-agers. So Hollywood is split between economics and art, with the odds by mere business calculation in favor of the former. Studios have to show profits, else studio heads fall.

Think of the good pictures that by measures of profit were failures or something close to it. Think, for instance, of *Twelve Angry Men, Sweet Smell of Success* and *A Face in the Crowd*. Superior films all, but not in the countinghouse. Take *The Gunfighter*, one of the best of the westerns, which was less than a smash because maybe—some assayers thought so—Gregory Peck went unshaven. Take, in more recent times, *The Diary of Anne Frank* and *The Big Country*.

The labor that goes into a movie strikes me as almost heroic. Such demands! A good script, if there is one, has been considered, reconsidered and perhaps amended time after time. The adjustments to budgets. The choice of location or locations. The casting. The management of actors and actresses, who aren't always easy to work with. The economic necessity of shooting scenes out of order, of skipping whole sequences and moving under cover if, say, the outdoor light isn't good. The endless takes, the re-enactments, that is, of bits of scene until at last one appears right. I have been on location and found the shooting not only dull but also immensely toilsome.

Whatever I've said or may say in its defense, Hollywood really isn't for me. I value my stout independence, though it is fragile, too much for surrender. I think it unhappy that studio contracts and swimming pools have seduced so many good writers. A one-shot deal justifies itself if you need the money. Then scuttle for home! Go back, if you value your writing, go back where you belong, to the work you belong in, remembering that good books endure.

The writer of novels and short stories, if I may speak for the craft, hits the mechanics of films with a bump. The bare-bone descriptions, told without grace. The always present tense. The interruptions of dialogue with camera directions too often insisted on and often and rightly discarded. The limitations of form that tend to keep films two-dimensional because there's no place for internal monologue unless the writer substitutes for it the old dodge of out-of-focus narration.

Afterwards, when the occasional screen-writer returns to his true work, he gets bumped again. It takes him a month or two, or even more, to assemble and employ the once familiar tools of his craft.

Yet he may have learned something. Hollywood can teach dialogue and pace and the significance of expression and movement. Which is to say that, as theater, it underscores showing.

Save for a few, I have no great admiration for actors and actresses. Though my firsthand observation is skimpy, I think of them as uninformed egotists, as compulsive exhibitionists. Then I remind myself that I too am an exhibitionist at one remove.

My impression of writers, producers, directors and story editors is different. I think back to a dozen or more that I came to know well. They gave brains and some direction to an enterprise whose compass always has been erratic. And they grew to be my ready and unselfish friends.

Though neither my books nor my screenplays, save *Shane*, came out as I hoped they would, I have no personal quarrel with Hollywood. I met nothing there but consideration, kindliness and generosity and would be false to myself were I fashionably snide. The wonder to me is that, from an industry so beset by difficulties, so many good pictures get made as do.

24

On the wall it was written that Montana was home. In 1953, when Helen was ready for high school, we moved there. Not in a single group, though, for I was under contract to Hecht-Hill-Lancaster and was working on *The Kentuckian*. In my absence my wife disposed of our Lexington house at a good price, saw to the packing and transportation of our household effects and made ready to start out by car. Never had I found moving so easy as when removed from the job by two or more thousand miles.

Some years before, we had bought as a vacation spot a section of rock-and-jackpine land near the mountains west of Choteau. On it were two cabins, some rickety outbuildings and a couple of ponds that rated as lakes in that semi-arid country. Now we bought a house in Great Falls and settled down, we thought, for good.

So I came home again, as nearly as a man can. It is always with a sense of loss that one returns to old and dear places. My vacations in Montana hardly had prepared me for the sum of change. In Choteau faces had vanished, names I knew best were forgotten, strangers had invaded the place. Even the geography—the mountains, fields, streams and woods where I had found adventure as a boy—seemed deprived and diminished. They were still there, but I, the boy, wasn't.

It was time's changes that gave me regret, not my removal. I had returned to my origins. If I belonged anywhere, save perhaps in Kentucky, I belonged in Montana. Yet I couldn't look at the state with complete pride. The newspaperman in me made me assess, and keeps me assessing, the good and the bad.

Montana counts an astonishing number of professional writers. Witness Dorothy Johnson, author of *The Hanging Tree*, and Dan Cushman, whose *Stay Away, Joe* no one should miss. And the state has and has had its painters, its sculptors and ceramists whose names and works are known afar. Yet the intellectual, even one as little tainted as I, finds the climate somewhat short of salubrious.

I cast about for reasons and doubtfully put first the item of communication, the low state of which is less a fault than an inevitability. Granted that the Anaconda Company's virtual monopoly of the daily press, now ended through sale after intolerable years, can be laid to weak popular will, the problem surpasses mere ownership. Our towns are small. Our cities, too. Small communities can't support big papers—which isn't to equate bigness with goodness—and, though little papers may be excellent, lack of space keeps them from being thorough.

Consider the situation, remembering that many a farm family as well as entire if tiny communities are beyond daily reach of a daily. Area, 147,138 square miles. Population, 674,767. Biggest city, Great Falls, with 55,357 people. From the closest really big cities, like Denver or Minneapolis, the Montanan can buy a fuller coverage of events and a variety of opinion—and get up to date a day or two late. There's radio, of course, and television, neither one everywhere within reach; but for all their importance they can't fill the vacuum.

It is a temptation to say that lack of communication, and that lack alone, distorts and confounds Montana politics and gives rigidity to choice. In any case the political view, though clear, is not enchanting. For a long time the state's two corporate giants, Anaconda and the Montana Power Company, virtually ruled the state. For reinforcements they looked to the cow counties east of the Continental Divide, where a belief in individuality and a man's rights extended to and made personal the impersonality of corporations. But there grew up the Farmers' Union, a formidable organization devoted to price supports, public power, cooperative endeavor and, in league with labor, to assaults on the companies and the capture of the Democratic party. For both sides economics comes ahead of party allegiance.

Two more nearly direct opposites could hardly be found, but there's the choice. The man of independent mind steers a lonely course between an American Legion mentality and that of the maddened man with the hoe and the handout. If he sides on occasion with the companies, he wears a copper collar; if on occasion he sides with the opposition, the F.B.I. ought to inquire into his loyalty.

Snobbery hardly exists in Montana. Race prejudice is infrequent save in diluted application to Indians and part-bloods of Indians and whites. Religious antagonisms are tame except in the direction of the communal Hutterite cult, whose members wear dowdy and uniform dress, refuse to bear arms, frown on education beyond the eighth grade, undersell local merchants with the fruits of their husbandry and by doctrine live in colonies apart from surrounding society. Yet a sort of anti-intellectual vigilanteism, an inhospitality to deviation, both in and beyond politics and economics, does exist. Difference all too often is suspect and unwelcome.

Having gone so far, I back up. In a state like Montana, where population is small and space great, human affairs are immediate and personal. Men are known for their sense of responsibility or their lack of it, and appraisals are easy as compared with the larger and harder assessments of faceless masses and the problems that masses present. The flashlight of Montana has a flashlight's narrow beam, picking out forms from the formless dark. Judgments vary with environment. And perhaps intellectual curiosity is proportionally as great here as elsewhere, but made to seem small because men are few.

And is communication, or the lack of it, the sole answer to what I have criticized in Montana?

"Lives without context," Jake Vinocur once said. He was a professor from Montana and a Jew from somewhere, possibly a ghetto where, for all I knew, lives could claim context.

We sat on the grass at my mountain home, under close stars, and around and away were the lights and shadows of a Montana night. It was an hour of no wind. Even the nearby aspens stood unworried, asleep without fret. On some far hill a coyote sang, deepening silence. And it seemed to me that Jake had put into three words all we had spoken.

This time was good, I thought, this time of silence and seeing, this rare time of felt union with the universe, these minutes escaped from a clock. Ahead and behind, first and last, to come and have come and gone—what were they? The past and the future and now, which wasn't now now, because it slid back in the thought of it, under eternal stars that might be under death sentences, too. Time was timeless and, by logic, then nothing, the great nothing that was the everything that was nothing. Minutes, days, months, years, centuries—they were no more than names, human inventions to mark the turn of a leaf and the swing of far suns. In timelessness existed the dead and the quick and the unborn, all in a context that Jake may or may not have meant to suggest.

"Today in Choteau," he said in his friendly, provocative way, "I stood on the street for a time, and a young woman in a convertible kept cruising the drag looking for something—something, I felt, she couldn't identify. But she kept driving back and forth, going slow, watching the sidewalks. What is it, Bud? An insufferable vacancy? The need of something to put between herself and the undertaker?" It was then that he said, answering himself, "Lives without context."

Now a breeze stirred, and the aspens danced anxiously, and I steered the talk toward my fruitless but somehow satisfying exploration of time.

"Maybe I follow you," I said. "No thought about precursors and successors, about relationships in the human adventure, about kinship to the dead and unborn and all that goes with it?"

Jake was silent, maybe examining what I had said, maybe thinking his own thoughts.

"About the sense of continuity in time, as if they considered the knowing and feeling of flow unrewarding and needless?"

He nodded, thinking beyond me, I thought.

We were talking about Montana, and we generalized, both knowing that our generalizations, true and false and tentative, applied to other of men's demarcations.

But we knew that new country, like Montana, had few really old fields to cherish. Less than a century ago there had been no Montana. There were no progenitors to relate past and present and future. We were a melting pot, melted quite well among native Americans, if there were any, and Germans and Irish and Danes and Welshmen and Norsemen and Jews and whatever others, yet not melted by history and ancestry into a flux. The shortage of attachments shortened the future to the next pay-off and the upcoming season; and the little bars in the little wheat-elevatored towns did a good business, and the juke boxes punished even deaf ears; and, come Saturday, that check that the bartender is holding will clear. Here was the now, isolated from old and unforeseen nows, the now by tongue just expressed and by time just sent to the past.

I was to think about lives without context again.

My guns had been stolen from my mountain cabin, my old guns, the examples of progress in firearms that had helped write whole chapters of American history. In the lot were a Kentucky, a Henry, one of the first of the Winchesters, a Sharps buffalo gun used in the battle of Adobe Walls, a single-shot Springfield like those that Custer's men died with, and several others, all of considerable value.

My friend, the sheriff, thought we might find them at Browning, agency town of the Blackfeet Indians.

From Choteau we drove north through country that was once the range of buffalo beyond counting, once the hunting grounds of a proud and indomitable tribe— indomitable, that is, before the white man introduced smallpox. Now the country was empty, or nearly so, great and

empty and aching. It stretched and rolled and tumbled before us in an immensity the mind couldn't embrace, flanked
to the westward by mountains that some deranged, palsied
artist had painted on the keen blue canvas of sky. The sheriff's car seemed a small thing for these miles.

Ways had changed, I thought, thinking about the theft
of the guns. Once upon a time a Western man might commit
the high crime of stealing a horse or the crime of stealing a
few beef, a crime not so high because the ostensible owner
might have branded a maverick or two in his time; but household possessions largely were safe and so left unguarded.
Cabin doors stayed unlocked against the need of some lost and
weary wayfarer. On winter nights the rancher, snug in his
house, put a light in a window as a signal of haven for any
shivering traveler. A box used to stand on the front counter
of Choteau's general mercantile store into which a man would
toss the key to the latch he'd just bought. To have kept it
would have been to disclose a shameful absence of faith.

And now my place had been entered and things had
been stolen, not just this once but one time before, when the
loot had been smaller. It was the work of kids, some people
said. Too many no-good juveniles were on wheels. Others
blamed breeds, meaning white-Indian hybrids. Others asked
darkly just who had seen my collection. I had closed my
mind to suspicion, believing it better to lose the guns than to
cloud the sun of my trust.

But the fact was there, standing in contrast to older
ways. Reasons suggested themselves. Mobility, for one. It
was no problem now to get far away from the scene of mis-
deed. And mere growth in human numbers levied its costs.
Neighbors widely separated had a sense of community that
communities lost. In any case it was too bad that doors had
to be locked, vain as my locking had been. I would have

chosen to have any door swing with the turn of a knob and to have in the house wood in the wood box and food on the shelf for the cold and the hungry.

Our quest came to nothing beyond admiration of old arms a lumberman had collected. The sleuthing completed, we went to a saloon and bought beers. Rather recently the federal government had sanctioned the sale of distillations and brews on the reservation, presumably on the incontestable grounds that the Indian's citizenship vested him with the right to a jag. A number of bars had sprung up, or squatted down, one like another.

The one we entered had a lively patronage and a record player turned up to the last endurable decibel. The customers were young people mostly, boys and girls of mixed blood, offspring of breeds like a score I had known, like scores in the harvest and hay fields and in calving and lambing sheds, who took their pay and got drunk and went broke and, as indifferent and seasonal workers, still thirsty, returned to the reservation, the place that was home.

The young couples danced with huge enjoyment and grace, danced the jitterbug instead of the old tribal steps, danced to the beat of a needle on wax, not to the thump of a stick on a hide, and over and over, between gulps of beer, they fed coins to the box for one song. It went:

> I've stayed around
> And played around
> This old town too long.
> Summer's almost gone.
> Yes, winter's comin' on.

And there were Jake and I, seated on the grass again, watching the stars. Lives without context. Lives without connections, excised from tradition, withered in the graft from red man to white. Lives unsure and fearful. Only there, back in Browning, within limits, in beery vacuum, was home.

We went out and started walking to the car. "Cold," the sheriff said, hunching into the wind. "Cold for this time of year."

: : : : : : : :

25

: : : : : : : :

Tom Larson died March 18, 1958.

Because until his last years I saw him infrequently, there's been small occasion so far to do more than mention him as an off-stage performer. Yet, like Mary Lizzie, he was a person who needs telling about.

To this day he's on stage to me as well as to others. When I travel the dizzying distances of Montana, when I visit the dry and sun-drenched towns or shiver in a Hudson's Bay chinook, when I look on what's left of abandoned endeavor, he fills me in. The dry forks of the Marias River shimmer away from us, the biggest land in the world. Cattle rustlers used to operate here, safe in the blind miles, and it isn't so far from here that Charles A. Buckley, alias Bow-

legs, died from a bullet fired in a saloon. Great drinker, his
killer. When he gave up booze, his patient wife gave him
up. Probably thought she was no use to him any more. It was
in that building, in Choteau, where Jake Schmidt, the tailor
doubling as coroner, held his first inquest and announced
that the hard-frozen dead man was in a damn bad fix. Used
to be a stage station here outside of Wolf Creek. Not much
left now to show for it. Rotten logs and the old trail dim in
the grass. Homesteaders probably made away with the
windows.

We go on in my recollections, combining in one trip
many we took together. Wasn't a fence to go through all the
sixty-odd miles to Great Falls when he rode a saddle horse
there from the ranch to hear William Jennings Bryan, way
back when. The Democratic delegation from Choteau, plug-
hatted, went in a surrey and changed teams at Langey's
Corners, but he got in ahead of the stylish boys and heard all
he wanted. On the way to Great Falls the Bryan train
stopped at Cascade, which was just thirty miles away and
almost deserted because of the rally, and Bryan went to the
rear platform and asked a seeming cowpuncher where all the
folks were, and the man answered, "Aw, they've gone to
Great Falls to hear some windjammer." The man was Charlie Russell, the artist. Up at the head of Mill Coulee Creek,
where mule-skinners with freight wagons used to stop for the
night, one of them was found dead. He was old man Edgar,
who couldn't read and, to moisten his whistle, had tapped a
keg marked WOOD ALCOHOL, DEADLY POISON. In buying Eva
Fox's old hook shop at Choteau as the site for its depot, the
Milwaukee Railroad sure picked a good spot—men were so
used to getting on and off there. Tom looks a little embar-
rassed. His sense of humor seldom enters the bedroom.

Tom came to Montana from Minnesota in 1895, fourteen years after his parents had migrated from an inland village in Norway, where he was born and had lived for six years. He was not a big man, though not really small, and, unlike the popular image, he was dark-skinned and dark-eyed, a black Norwegian as Norwegians say. He was a graduate, approximately, of the fourth grade.

He brought with him curiosity, wit, a willingness to take chances, an expectation that excluded both despair and regret and an assurance far more becoming than cocky. He was nineteen when a bartender asked him if he was of age. "I've had the seven-year itch three times," he answered, and the bartender drew him a beer.

In those early years he did what he found to do, always with an eye fixed ahead. At one time or another he drove stage from Collins to Choteau, bought, broke and sold horses, served as county assessor, kept a country store. The store was a nip-and-tuck enterprise. Often he couldn't pay the bills from suppliers. When he couldn't, he put the check for one creditor in an envelope addressed to another, knowing that each would return the payment and call respectful attention to his mistake. Thus, in those days of slow delivery, he gained three or four weeks in which to build up his bank balance. That was the closest to sharp practice I ever knew him to come.

As a start on the ranch he hoped to establish, he filed on a government-owned gravel bar that other land-seekers, ignorant of its possibilities as irrigated hay meadow, had scorned. He called the place Camp Easy, though the name seems appropriate only with reference to his laundry, which he hung on a wire strung in his irrigation ditch. Horses were his first interest. At one time, to use Western terminology, he owned forty brands and went with carloads of the broncs he'd rough-broken to markets in Indiana and the Deep South. As times changed and his acreage grew, he turned from horses to sheep and cattle, switching from one to the other according to circumstance. With another man he undertook the construction of a big irrigation canal from the Muddy River to open land around the present-day town of Brady, which he founded. Before he was through, he owed $70,000, a staggering sum at that time, so distressing to the bank that had seen no way out but to keep financing him that he transferred his account to a more confident house. But the project had the results he had foreseen. Landseekers were eager to pay for water rights in the canal. Water meant surer crops. More important, it entitled a man to file on three hundred and twenty acres, or twice what he could stake out without it. Tom paid back the bank and left on deposit a sizable profit. And today, looking on the irrigated fields, you know he wasn't the only winner.

Tom was a poor politician, having little memory for names and no room in his character for blandishments, deals and evasions, but he spent a record twenty-one years in the Montana Senate. He got to know every Montanan, it seemed, even if names often eluded him, and everybody got to know him. He became an expert in parliamentary procedure and a sharp-shooter as an opponent, a laconic reducer to the ridiculous of disliked propositions. By and by people began to refer to him as The Little Giant because he killed so many bills, or had a hand in killing them. One he did away with would have enlarged the place of music in the public schools. He thought the bill beyond curricular proportions and its appropriation beyond Montana's means. From the floor he asked its advocate, a musician, if he would yield for a question. The senator would. "What instrument do you play?" Tom asked. The man answered, "The piccolo." Tom let himself back in his seat, saying, "That's all I wanted to know."

Some quality or qualities—sense of humor, incorruptibility, geniality, slowness on his part to take offense—saved him from assault and made him a friend of friend and foe alike. It tickled him to recall an incident that had tickled rather than offended him in fact. Years before, when settled Montanans were showing some resentment at the great Norwegian invasion, he went into a bar and ordered a drink. The only other customer was an Irish sheepherder happily named Shorty McGorty, who was unhappily affected by the sight of the newcomer. "You know," he said to the bartender for Tom's benefit, "we got to watch out or them goddam, piss-poor North Sea Chinamen are goin' to take over."

Some time afterwards Tom stepped out of a saloon and paused on the walk to look across the street, where workmen were erecting Choteau's most ambitious building. Watching, he puffed on a cigar. The preacher whose butt my father had threatened to kick saw Tom swing from the hellhole and caught sight of the cigar.

The preacher thumbed toward the saloon. "Brother," he asked, "do you go in there often?"

"Often as I like," Tom said.

"To drink?"

"When I feel like it."

The preacher pointed to the cigar. "How many of those do you smoke a day?"

"Many as I want."

"Brother," the preacher said, waving toward the construction across the street, "if you didn't drink and didn't smoke, maybe someday you could put up a building like that."

Tom puffed on his cigar. He asked, "Do you drink?"

"Of course not. Never."

Tom took the cigar from his mouth. "Ever try one of these?"

"No, Brother. It's wrong."

"Well," Tom said, "if you change your ways, maybe someday you can put up a building. I'm putting up that one over there."

He was, too. It remains the most substantial building in Choteau, though built in about 1917.

In his spur-of-the-moment facility for saying the unexpected, for putting wit and essential sense into a capsule, he belonged in the company of Will Rogers, Charlie Russell and other gifted old-timers now mostly dead. He came home very wobbly one night after a reunion with out-of-town cronies. In the bedroom adjoining her room Mother Larson heard him bumping around. Next morning over the breakfast table she said, "You must have had quite a load on last night." Tom speared another flapjack, "Yes," he answered. "Should've made two trips."

We had a custom, he and I, of going out on the town one night during each of my summer vacations. Once, at about midnight, we decided we'd had enough and were about to take leave when a party of friends sailed in and hove to. So general is the practice of treating in small Montana saloons that drinks were ranged around us almost before we said no. "Pretty rugged," I said to Tom the next day. He nodded and asked, "How many did we have after we quit?"

He was an easy touch for the shiftless, no matter that few ever repaid him. One, obviously thirsty, once asked for the loan of ten dollars. Tom said he had just half that much in his pocket. Handing it over, he commented, "This way we'll both save five dollars."

At the risk of distortion—he was a good drinking man but far from a drunk—I'll tell two more stories that come from the cup.

He and Mother Larson were guests at our summer camp in Montana. From inside the cabin I saw him drop down on the grass. He put his hat on the ground and parked his cigar in its crease. Only trouble could make him act in a manner so foreign, and I ran out and asked what was the matter. He didn't answer. He sat pale and hunched, with some agony in him. Mother Larson came up, and Harriet, and we urged him to go with me to a doctor. He kept shaking his head. The ladies disappeared briefly, and I suggested a drink, though gin was all I had left. He swallowed the immense hooker I brought him and by and by indicated that a second might help. He was back on his feet when the ladies returned, his hat on his head and his cigar reinstated.

"You wanted me to go to a doctor," he said, "and come to find out, all I needed was a saloon."

Maybe he got what a doctor would have ordered. One of them guessed afterwards that he had kidney colic, which alcohol would have relieved by dilation.

It was a year or more from that time that Tom and I overcelebrated in Kentucky the coming of the new year. He was up and smoking when I wavered down from upstairs. "Tom," I said, holding my head, "don't you hate yourself this morning?"

"Hate myself?" He looked at me in honest astonishment. "Why should I hate myself? Tom Larson's the best friend I ever had."

It struck me later that he had put into two sentences all that Joshua L. Liebman had managed in an entire book, *Peace of Mind*, and more than Norman Vincent Peale had put in another.

When he was festive, he could be persuaded to sing,
though he had a voice that might have matured in a swamp.
Tone and key didn't matter to his rapt listeners: the words
he croaked were words not heard before unless from him. The
number most in demand went:

Three Hebrews they were talking
About when they would die,
But they were undecided
As to where they'd like to lie.
Isaac picked Jerusalem.
New York for Rubenstein.
But when it came to Cohen,
He said, "The place for mine
"Is where old Shannon's flowing.
"That's where I would repose,
"In an Irish cemetery
"With a shamrock on my nose.
"And the devil will be trying
"To find me, I suppose,
"But he'll never think of looking
"Where the River Shannon flows."

When Tom was nearing eighty, Harriet and I decided
to give a birthday party for him, a stag affair to which we'd
ask his diminished circle of aging friends throughout the
state. For the first time in long association he seemed timid,
as if the years had worn his old assurance thin. He called the
idea foolish. He refused to help with the guest list. If we
insisted on a party, all right, he guessed he'd have to come,
but he wouldn't make a speech. No, sir!

We went ahead.

To set the stage, two qualities of Tom's need mention.
Ordinarily, no matter who his company, his speech was

clean, almost free of the words the West so often uses freely. He was a Republican, true-blue, branded-in-the-hide, right-wing Republican, doctrinal fellow of Hoover and Goldwater. For the record if not the story, add that he could smell mischief from afar and had no time for Joe McCarthy or such hysterics as are banded now under Birch's banner.

His timidity vanished fast when he got to the party. Here were old friends, old partners and mellowed opponents in politics, old roundup riders, sheepmen and cattlemen, some not seen for years. Here was good talk, revived times and old bourbon.

They drank and they talked and they ate, and each in his turn got up from the table and saluted The Little Giant. And Tom, after all, did want to speak.

After a little uncertainty he got around to his years in the Senate, to companions there and maneuverings and the struggles for sanity in legislation against the insane men of the left.

"We called them Bolsheviks then," he said, "but that name's died out. Now they're Progressives." He put a match to his cigar and waved it out and then removed the cigar and waved it, too. "Bolsheviks. Progressives," he went on—and found his finish. "Some of them Bolsheviks was so progressive they wiped their ass before they shit."

He lived his life generously, or, to put it more accurately, he was generous to life, as life by and large was generous to him—a reciprocity, it could almost be believed, that he took as a matter of course. In funds or in debt he went openhanded, without conceit or complaint. No public cause found him clutching his money. He gave to all the churches in town, saying in light explanation that if one road didn't take him to heaven maybe another would. The lock box opened after his death held a sheaf of promissory notes.

They represented only a part of the money he'd loaned and never got back. Yet never in memory did he dun his debtors. He assumed a man was as good as his word, as he was himself. If the man wasn't, oh, well. The judgments he made of men untrustworthy in any direction were hardly vocal. Even the inquirer received only a subdued word or two and had to know Tom to know the finality of his verdict.

Our birthday party was the last one for Tom, as we had feared it would be. Even then he was failing and had been for months. The legs that had carried him jaunty and straight for so long needed the help of a cane. One eye was blind after an unsuccessful cataract operation, and the light was growing dim in the other, and he drove his car, slowly in low, only the short blocks to Main Street and back. Other drivers recognized man and machine and, out of solicitude far more than for safety, pulled to the curbs to leave the way open. Only his mind remained vigorous, contradicting as always a remark that amuses me in self-application. He had reported a sleepless night, and I asked him if he didn't dislike just to lie in bed thinking. "I don't lie there and think," he answered. "I just think I'm thinking."

Month by inevitable month he grew frailer after the party. And it was as if he couldn't understand or accept the fact that a constitution that had served him so well for so many years should let him down now. He was perplexed by it, and put out. He didn't talk much of death beyond saying once, with an inelegance he may have used for a cover, "One of these days I got to croak." He seemed unwilling to go, rather than frightened. In his largely silent, sick presence one imagined what was going on in his head. Life had been good, and he loved it. This earth had been good, it was plenty good, and he loved it. Granted a heaven somewhere, why move? Why must he move? He was satisfied here.

He had to go to the hospital again, for the last time, we knew; and most of us close to him gathered round, making light talk before the ambulance came. With that false cheer, in that compulsion to speak, even of nothing, that doom generates in those guilty of health, I said, "Quite a delegation, Tom. Most of the tribe here."

"Yeah," he said, and a wrinkle of smile touched his face. "A goin'-away party."

: : : : : : : :

26

: : : : : : : :

George Jackson lost his mother early in life and became almost a member of our household. He had no gift for books, or rather, small interest, and Father would have snorted more than he did if all of us hadn't liked him so much. In hours off from high school he learned to barber and, after graduation, entered the trade.

During the years I lived in Great Falls, it was my habit, when bound for Twin Lakes, to stop at Choteau and call at the barbershop. I liked to be with him and he with me, and more often than not he would say that business was lousy, so lousy he would lock up the shop and accompany me to the cabin. It should be added that he was my foremost advocate and no doubt wore his customers out by repeated references to me and my work.

One summer night we set forth, supplied with vegetables and choice beef and a bottle. Three miles short of port my old Plymouth stalled, its generator having grown impotent. We dug out the jug with solicitude and, forsaking all else, started walking.

Rather, we stumbled, for the night had no sky and the earth no suggestion of shape. The gravel road was a ghost of a ribbon, made tricky with invisible stones. In this dark, owls and bats would have crashed.

It seemed sound shortly to halt a moment and have a nip from the jug, and we did and went on, careful of our cargo, and nipped again, and again; and I began to see lines and hear rhythms in almost total recall. So, at a stop, I recited "Mr. Flood's Party." George said it was appropriate. He liked "The Song of Wandering Aengus," too, as well as Shakespeare and Frost and Housman, those old book friends of mine whose verses stood clear in the dark.

We reached my turn-off, and the cabin was just over a knoll, and the night lifted a little, showing the jagged line of the Rockies; and here was Robinson speaking through me again.

> Dark hills at evening in the west,
> Where sunset hovers like a sound
> Of golden horns that sang to rest
> Old bones of warriors under ground,
> Far now from all the bannered ways
> Where flash the legions of the sun,
> You fade—as if the last of days
> Were fading, and all wars were done.

George set the bottle down and grabbed my arm. "Good God, Buddy," he said, "is all that yours?"

I picked up the bottle, and we threaded the cattle pass into my place and went on to the cabin.

Once in late April when the air smelled of spring, we went to Twin Lakes for a relaxed and pleasant weekend, imagining that a good share of our time would be spent out of doors. That very night it began to snow. Next morning the fall measured sixteen inches. We tried to get the car to the brow of a wind-swept hill, but it gave out when some two tons of snow had pushed up in front of it. The next morning we found that five more inches had fallen.

But we had firewood enough, though I had to flounder out and cut it by hand while George, who had grown too fat for exercise much more demanding than the manipulation of clippers, fussed around in the kitchen. And we had plenty of food on the shelves and in the deepfreeze. More, we had poker chips and a worn deck of cards. What if we were snowbound? Business, I told George, was probably lousy.

The words did not ease him. Much more than I, he was a town man, though he hadn't been very far to the east or west or north or south of Choteau. Always, after a day or two in the country, he wanted to see signs saying EATS and DRUGS and BAR and GASOLINE. So now, though he didn't say why, he kept itching, kept looking out the window at the deep-covered landscape and the car that was only a hump in the snow.

Sunday afternoon the dreary flakes began to fall again. We were playing pitch, but George's thoughts weren't on the cards. He stared outside, and the snow thickened, and at last he turned to me and asked gravely, "Buddy, what are your plans for tomorrow?"

John Starr, then senior editor for McGraw-Hill, came to Great Falls. We had common business, that of signing up authors for The American Trails Series, of which I was nominally editor-in-chief. One of the men we wanted was Dan Cushman, my fellow-townsman.

I thought John and Dan ought to get well acquainted, to have undisturbed opportunity to talk over the project; and it struck me that Twin Lakes was the right place for the purpose. We could take steak and potatoes and other camp fare, and something to lubricate tongues. John and Dan were agreeable, and at Choteau George said again that business was lousy. He pulled down the shades and locked up the shop.

George, a better than fair cook, specialized in fried potatoes and onions, which, by God, under no circumstances could be put on the fire at the same time because the onions would burn before the potatoes were ready. Meticulously he undertook his assignment, a glass at his side, while I saw to the steaks and the peas.

John and Dan were in a friendly, close huddle at the kitchen table. Things were working out fine, I thought as I glanced at them. Agreement was coming to pass. George looked their way often and kept an ear cocked. Time came to turn the potatoes, and he turned them and marched to the conference table, full of importance.

"Now see here, boys," he said, "let's not talk shop."

They quit.

On the way back to Choteau John Starr got to praising an anthology, in translation, of Latin-American verse. One poem had affected him particularly. He quoted one line, then a second and third.

"I am partly moon and partly traveling salesman."

He gave us time to think the line over. Like him, I was struck by it, by the spare imagery that captured the mixture of heaven and soil in all of us.

"My speciality is finding hours
Which have lost their watches."

I didn't have time to say amen, for George broke in. "It's a bunch of baloney," he declared. "Even if I understood it, I would still say it's a bunch of baloney."

Later, Dan Cushman, who did write a Trails book, said George was the only one who made sense that night.

I had just completed the manuscript of *These Thousand Hills*, and again George and I were batching it at Twin Lakes. Out of California a call came from Ben Benjamin of Famous Artists, my agents. Arthur Kramer, then story editor for Twentieth Century–Fox, wanted to see the manuscript before publication. He would fly to Great Falls and meet me, if that was all right. It was more than all right.

My Helen and I drove to the airport. Kramer emerged from the plane, a slight man, tastefully dressed, who seemed mildly astonished that we should have taken the trouble to meet him. He had the Jewish gentlemen's gentle manner, which I think far more characteristic of Jews than the racists' stereotype.

In the long evening twilight my wife and daughter and I took Kramer into the country I had been writing about. Inevitably we wound up at Choteau. In the American Legion bar we encountered friends, including Tom Larson, who waved his cigar and ordered drinks for the table. Kramer was quiet and unassuming and seemed too well-tailored for this bunch. He looked rather startled when the bartender, out of old friendship, said to me, "Well, if it ain't the smart-ass writer!"

George Jackson wasn't present but presently entered, having lifted a few on the way. I introduced him to Kramer, about whose name and arrival he had grown fuzzy.

George asked, "What's the name again?"

A transplanted Easterner, Kramer didn't pronounce

his name with the stress on r's that Montanans are used to.

George was puzzled but all at once understood and put a faithful foot forward for me. "Glad to see you, Art!" The word for his voice was robust. "How are you, Cougar?"

Cougar accepted a hearty hand, though he appeared somewhat dazed. Yet he must have enjoyed himself: a year or so afterwards he was proposing a return to Montana.

Kramer flew home, after evincing some pride in his new monicker, and George and I were again at the cabin when the telephone rang. Ben Benjamin on the other end. Twentieth Century–Fox had made a firm offer of seventy-five thousand for movie rights. Would I accept?"

"Seventy-five thousand," I said. "I don't know, Ben. The book isn't even out yet. If it succeeds, it might sell for more."

Ben sounded discouraged.

While he was talking, I looked at George, who had a far-away light in his eyes, as if he were dividing seventy-five thousand by haircuts at one-fifty each.

"Tell you what," I told Ben. "Make it a hundred thousand flat, and I'll settle."

Ben's tone suggested I had asked the impossible, but he said he would call back next day.

George began smoking cigarettes, one after another. His eyes and face, indeed his whole manner, said I was a fool. Once he sighed, "Goodbye to a fortune, Buddy."

There was work to do that next day. Winter was almost at hand, and Twin Lakes had to be buttoned up— canoe put away, lawn furniture stored, headgate shut off, wood stacked in the woodbox, poison replenished for mice, beds to be unmade and blankets hung up on lines, outbuildings to be examined and locked. George wouldn't help me. No, sir, he would stay near the phone.

The call was late. George sat tense as I listened. The studio had agreed to my figure.

George clapped his hands as I replaced the receiver. "Goddam it," he shouted. "I knew you'd make it. I just knew you would."

He overcelebrated that night.

A wise young acquaintance of mine once said: You don't have to define or state reasons for friendship. Friendships exist, and that's that.

It happened that George was present at Twin Lakes when my old dog, Coney Island Hot Dog the Second, was dying. A stroke had felled her, and she lay on her side, by degrees dying down to the tail she wanted to wag, dead save for her eyes' recognition, dead save for her gentle and trustful eloquence of expression.

It seemed to me, watching her, that I was saying goodbye to memories stored through the years. Goodbye to the time my girl child chose her out of a litter of dachshunds and later dressed her in doll clothes and forever remained proud of her pick. Goodbye to the day she was skunked up, to the day she fell into the pit of the privy while chasing a pack rat, to the afternoon she tackled a porcupine and got quills in her nose and cried at our cruelty in pliering them out. Goodbye to what she expected, by look and by bark, knowing we were omnipotent. Goodbye to a dependence I had come to depend on. Goodbye to a part of Twin Lakes.

George, who was fond of her, too, did what I couldn't do. He carried her out to his car and drove the twenty-three miles to Choteau and had the veterinarian there put her away. He brought her back, wrapped in her blanket, and in uncertain tones told me she had died quickly once the needle was in her.

As my young acquaintance had said, you don't have to have a reason for friendship.

27

Why, if my gaze is even half focused, do I choose to live
in a state of which I'm critical in the directions I've mentioned? As I start to count the becauses, I become fidgety.
Maybe a writer should not come to terms with his environment. Maybe he writes more and better in recalled happiness, away from what pleases him, present only in retrospect.
Elsewhere I might have worked harder; elsewhere, where I
might have felt homesick, deprived and forlorn, I might have
reached farther. In almost ten years I haven't done much. A
stint or two in Hollywood. In a series of novels one book,
These Thousand Hills—which was my most difficult and
least successful because it dealt with the cowpuncher and had
to avoid, if it could, the stylized Western myth. A collection

of short stories. A handful of magazine pieces. Less than a handful of verses.

I haven't worked hard enough and advance as excuse, as most writers do with some justice, that I don't know when I'm working. If I get stuck on a page, the way out may come to me while I'm shaving.

The question stands: Why am I here?

I like Montana, and I like Montanans. Most of my people, aside from their certain rigidities, are agreeable and generous and in person engaging. The rancher in a pickup stops to ask if he can help you with a flat. The old-timer, his youth renewed by hundred-proof, talks of his friend, the history of just yesterday. The moneyed man plays poker with his barber and asks him home to take pot luck. So it's been a bad year? What the hell? Another season's coming up. The bartender, just presented to a giant of a man, says cordially, "Jesus Christ! You're big enough to eat hay." The chambers of commerce, confusing size with quality and in that delusion tendering sugar tits to industry, can still brag of the fish and game that only uncongestion can account for.

Time and adjustment and liking and my sense of context. The mind-heard echoes of old trappers on the beavered streams. The grind of prairie schooners. A buffalo skull in a wallow. The time-gentled melancholy of the first homesteaders, forced to leave the sunsets. An arrowhead shining in the gravel after rain. All these and more.

Mountain water over shining rock, which DeVoto said he loved the best of all. Stars like bonfires. Clouds swelling in the bellies of the peaks in Glacier Park. A cottontail at the edge of a thicket. A horseman and a bronc. Old Chief Big Lake's grave on a benchland facing westward over the valley of the Teton. Fishing streams and one trout rising to my

Royal Coachman, and my not caring much if it should get away. A bar of song remembered from some country schoolhouse dance. The wild geese V-ing, shouting their adventure. A buck's antlers through the quaking asp. The first men here and the things they saw that I see now. The coyotes calling.

A different, a less harried, a more open and a better world. My world?

April in Montana is a harsh and fretful month, a time of wayward winds and unpredicted snows and rains as cold as snow. If the sun shines for a day or two or three, the eager willows swell, and sap warms the wintered aspens in the foothills, and magpies start building nests like twiggy basketballs—but all too early, all too soon. Snow will come again, and cold, and the reaching grasp at new life be discouraged and postponed. Ordinarily, that is.

It is the last of April, and we have just had a big snow which, after a dry winter, is good for grass and wheat but bad for birds and buds. Even now there is a touch of storm in the air, and the sun, after trying to shine, seems ready to give up.

I am at Twin Lakes, looking more often out a quartsized picture window than at this waiting page. The place is a pocket in the great eastern apron of the Rockies, and I have kept the unimaginative name, not wanting to monkey with history even if I could persuade people to indulge my monkeyshines.

I am alone, but when I look down at the floor I see my old dead dog again. She hates cold and misty-moist weather and gazes up with pleading eyes, knowing I am God and could change things if I would. I dislike to disappoint her. All gods must feel regretful.

It is good to be alone, though lonely, while the fire in the old range crackles and gladdens bones as furnace fires and fanned electric heat cannot. It is good to think, to sit and think or just to think you're thinking, to let come to mind what will—convictions, fancies, the bigs and littles of experience and fragments of a dance tune danced to long ago. And here you are, the product of what has gone before; yet not all of it can account for the you that you've become. And yet, I think, and not for nothing altogether: the blue hen's chick.

A few days more, and I shall wish for people and routine and someone to do the dishes, but now I find release in living as I please, alone, erratic and untidy, and in working as I please, with books and papers and unanswered letters scattered around me and discarded pages under foot. I have a hunch that all clean desks have littered drawers. It is good to be away from noise and the barbiturate temptation of TV, to be free of outside rule and expectation. Internal fret is fret enough.

Outside, the snow is melting but the sky still overcast. Clouds obscure Ear Mountain, but I know it rises there, four miles away, and on brighter days will bolster me again. The green grass shows on the shoveled path beyond the window, and birds are feeding on the grain that I have scattered. Now is the season of the junco, the Oregon snowbird. In sight are some two dozen of them, perky little creatures, smaller than English sparrows, with dark hoods pierced by white beaks and marks of rusty red on backs and sides. They arrive to feed as if on signal and on signal wing away, shortly to return together. Something about the window keeps confusing them as it does not other birds. Four or five have hit it, leaving bits of down on the glass, and one lay shut-eyed and gasping afterwards. I went out and picked him up and brought him in and, though confident of his identity, checked him against my key to birds. In an hour he got his breath and vision and fluttered hot-pulsed in my palm and on release set out uncertainly.

A yellowheaded blackbird, a rare sight at this altitude, just made a landing on the path, brilliant in his gold and ebony against the farther snow. Out toward the woodpile six or seven magpies are shouting grace for fare left there. A solitary chipmunk munches something on the fence rail. I cannot see the home lake from my makeshift desk but know a greenhead and a lady mallard are making love off shore and that a goldeneye, resplendent for his courting, cruises with his mate.

We shall have young life around the place again this year. Not only ducklings. Magpies, the smartest of our birds. White-crowned sparrows. Pine squirrels. Flickers. Clark's nutcrackers. Every season squirrels and flickers fight for homes in one old hollow aspen. Hard to say which side will win. Sometimes one does, sometimes the other. Already the great horned owls that like the north lake have hatched their broods. Perhaps I should say brood, for I don't know that more than one pair nests there. One pair does, though, and has for year on year—the only Twin Lakes birds to mate before the Ides of March.

Cottontails a cup would cover will explore our world, their eyes fluid with wonder, and a doe will lead her fawn to a salt block on the hill, and in the early mornings the marmots will be out. The tramp black bear of last year may recommence his rounds. With luck we'll see a mountain lion. No sweat. We go unmolested, without arms.

Interruption.

I just shot a skunk.

I'm always glad of interruptions. They take me from

the typewriter, and I find excuses for not coming back.
Well, tomorrow will be another day and, from the looks of
things, one like today.

The skunk—a male, I think, but, male or female, not
an it because animals aren't its to one withdrawn from human
company—he came poking round the woodpile, nosing for
the scraps that I had left for magpies. When I went out he
spread his black and white and stomped his front feet, warning that he'd pivot and perfume me if I dared another step.
At my retreat he ambled off with fine contempt, poised pos-
sessor of world power. I put shells in my twenty-gauge and
followed him and shot. Usually a skunk, dying, releases a
defiant charge. This one didn't. With all his powers he fell
and lay, his farewell to the world unfired.

Not until late years did skunks invade my country. We
had assumed we were too high for them. They came, though,
perhaps as a consequence of great increases lower down. I
incline to think their thriving may be due in part to the
proud war waged on coyotes by experts of the state and
nation, for there is evidence that coyotes, though daunted by
grown skunks, still feast on those newborn.

A skunk is more than a nuisance, to watch for in the
dark, to call your pup away from if you can. An egg- and
chick-eater, he is the first destroyer of ground birds. Give him
free rein, and larks and sparrows, prairie chickens, pheas-
ants, grouse and even ducks will thin out and maybe disappear. That he is a mouser, too, is not atonement for his
sins.

The animals I trap or shoot or poison I kill reluctantly,
in the hard knowledge that I should or must.

Take that noisome little clown, the pack or trade rat.
Once inside your cabin—and he'll get there if you don't

watch all openings, including the dampers on your stove—
he'll wreak havoc while, with merry thumps of tail, he beats
out his vandal's glee. He'll soil, he'll chew, he'll steal, he'll
hide his loot and leave behind a stench impervious to all the
vaunted hosts of cleansers and deodorants.

I can say nothing for the porcupine except, when I
consider his figure and fecundity, that love indeed must con-
quer all. He's stupid. He's destructive. He thrashes his
cruelly needled tail without discrimination, into the faces of
dogs, who go insane with pain and fury, and against the
velvet noses of merely curious calves and colts and often older
livestock. Unattended, the quills may strike the brain or cen-
tral nervous system, for they are feathered to work deep.
First, though, unable to suckle or to graze for the stubbled
torture in their muzzles, ranch animals may starve unless
detected, locked in a squeeze and operated on with pliers.
Some great authority will have to tell me how porcupines
contribute to nature's equilibrium.

Pack rats and porcupines and skunks—these I destroy,
and one other creature that I hate to most of all. That is the
beaver.

I see him every summer, for he keeps insisting that my
premises are his. I see the quiet V he wedges in the lake at
sundown. I hear the hard smack of his tail as, startled, he
submerges. I spot him on the shore, braced by his tail, chip-
ping at a lovely aspen with teeth like sharp and highly tem-
pered chisels. I see his winter store of severed saplings, set
under water in the mud close by his house. I see and, seeing,
know this gentle creature will have to be removed.

Given less time than even I with my experience can
think, he'll lay waste an aspen grove. A neurosis afflicts him.
Like the human layers-waste of forests, though with more
mystic motivation, he has to be logging, whether downed

trees serve the purposes of food or dams or not. He has to be as busy as a beaver and, under this compulsion, is as dedicated as any bureaucrat. More, like the Corps of Engineers or the brass of Reclamation, he can't endure the sight of running water. So he clogs not only streams, with sometime benefit, but irrigation ditches that, dammed, could never contribute to power or navigation. Ten times or more a summer he crams his cuttings in the round-holed headgate that lets a ditch into my lake, though not the best of dams there would create a pond. It is enough for him, an engineer, that he slow or stop the flow.

But still I like to watch him and feel poorer when I shoot him or take him from a trap.

It used to be the animals and I had privacy. Eight hundred acres, no matter that they're poor, provided range enough. We could roam and run and take a dip, knowing that the sky, eccentric though it might be, was free of peering eyes. Now planes spy on us and take pictures, I suppose, always by my impression when the human hiker halts his steps on nature's orders and stands or squats exposed; and their drone in any case is alien and unwelcome, remindful of the fact that progress leaves us no retreat. Not often but too often they are Forest Service planes and private kites; and yesterday there came a jet. So perfected that it can't work up a sweat within the speed of sound, it broke the barrier with its synthetic thunderclap and upset the animals and me and shook the bones of this old cabin, which seemed to me to whimper all night long while the west wind tried to soothe it. Old things ought not to be shook up. Price of survival, the smooth brass of the Air Force tells us smoothly.

The jet cleaved the air, leaving against the unoffending sky the white cut of its swipe. I watched it out of sight, hoping it would fall on a scientist.

In a wild moment once I undertook to underscore, by means of a hillbilly song, my hoary and admittedly excessive attitude. This humdinger was to be the cry of a mountain man like me—who wanted space and air, but folks moved about, and as folks do they bred a crew till only the air was bare.

Hiatus here because, after this infirm beginning or something close to it, I skipped the next and connecting verse and, under a strong wind, sailed into the chorus. It went this way:

Keep them jaybirds outta my sky,
Where only birds was meant to fly,
And the Lord on High
Says you're coming too nigh.
Keep them noisy, nosey, pyznus jimcracks
Outta my sky!

At this point I decided the task was beyond my talents, and, anyhow, my case was long since lost.

Better than drawing boards, test flights and test explosions, I like the military preparations said to have been pursued by a loser in the Riel or Cree Rebellion up north in Canada some eight decades past. He slipped across the line into Montana and with him somehow slipped nine squaws. His intention: to breed a family fighting force so numerous as to right the wrong. Of course the war was never waged, but the man tried mightily, so mightily that hereabouts and nowadays a man can hardly number the fruits of his endeavors.

Gazing out the window toward my fence line, I feel a twinge, residual from history and myth, because I don't raise something here, but let Nature take her course instead. Not much of this rock-and-jackpine country recommends itself for cultivation, but there's a spot or two where hardy garden stuff would grow if the grower fenced and garrisoned the garden against sneak attacks by cottontails and black-tailed deer and mountain gophers. But I'd rather walk than hoe, rather recognize wild flowers than weed tame turnips. Coral root, an orchid of a sort, rises colored in the aspen grove, like asparagus with apoplexy, and Indian paintbrush blows, and on the flats in season the yellow loco lifts its deep-piled carpet above the modest carpet of the carpet flowers. And I delight in knowing among what I'm cast, delight in surely saying this plant is this, that animal that, and here a deer survived its journey through the night.

But still the sturdy yeoman, who plows not but only watches and from time to time puts labored words on paper. Who asks not for handouts either, for growing or not growing. What did happen to yesterday's stout yeoman?

A new arrival, a redpoll, not so jaunty as the juncos, feeds with them on the path, feeds unafraid and unmolested, his Roman red respected. And two bronze grackles, male and female, lower flaps and come to earth. No jolts. No taxiing. Perfect, runless, two-point landings. Unconcerned with other birds, they peck and preen. One preens, that is. The male, not yet allowed by her to sow, reaps a tame oat and then extends his wings and spreads his tail and flutters all his feathers and, that display done, cocks his white eyes at the sky as if asking heaven when. The show-off ritual, the beginning ritual of love.

Idly, while I've watched, I've wondered what I want, where I stand and what's my doctrine. A simple answer came, though the years have taken part of its fulfillment.

To lean but, more important, to be leaned on,
For that's what friendship's for.

To be loved but to love,
Or what's the use?
To be generous toward life,
Else I lose myself.
Above all else, to care!

Suddenly the yard is bare, abandoned by the birds, left vacant at the last by the chipmunk after he had flirted good-night from the woodpile; and I feel deserted and thrown in on myself, as if I were the last of life.

Westward, astride the backbone of the Rockies, the sun sets through the mist. Time to have a drink. To have two, maybe. Almost time, as old-time camp cooks used to say, to burn a mulligan.

End of an April day.

On the south fork of the Teton River, outside of Choteau, Montana, 1912. Left to right: Chick Guthrie, Bud Guthrie, A. B. Guthrie, Sr.

Chick Guthrie and Bud Guthrie, about 1914–15

A. B. Guthrie, Jr., as fire patrol, 1921

At the *Lexington Leader,* early 1930s. Left to right: Dan Bowmar,
Joe Jordan, A. B. Guthrie, Jr.

Neiman class, Harvard University, 1945

A. B. Guthrie, Jr., with his file cards for *The Big Sky,* 1947

Guthrie with his wife, Harriet, and son, Bert, 1947

On the trip down the Missouri River, 1950. Left to right: William Lederer, Major Williams, Guthrie, Bernard De Voto

Bread Loaf Writer's Conference, 1950s. Robert Frost is in back row, center.
Front row, extreme left: John Ciardi; center: Guthrie;
extreme right: William Sloan

Guthrie and his daughter, Helen, on the Ohio River near Louisville, 1966

Bud and Carol Guthrie at The Barn, 1976. Photograph by Jay Fowler

The family in the kitchen of The Barn, 1980. Left to right: Herb Luthin, Carol and Bud Guthrie, Amy Luthin

A. B. Guthrie, Jr., in his study at The Barn with Miles Gaede, 1988.
Photograph by Marc Gaede

AFTERWORD

Alfred Bertram Guthrie, Jr.—1901–1991.
A Remembrance

By David Petersen

Bud Guthrie was my friend, my mentor, and remains a signifi-
cant character in my life. Thus I am deeply honored to have been
asked to write the following summary of his life and career subsequent to the publication of *The Blue Hen's Chick* in 1965. For
keeping me on a straight factual line, I owe a debt of thanks to
Carol Guthrie.

"Suddenly," Bud Guthrie says in the final paragraphs of his autobiography, "the yard is bare . . . and I feel deserted and thrown
in on myself, as if I were the last of life. . . . End of an April day."
     These sentiments carry the unmistakably bittersweet scent
of melancholy. I finished my first reading of *The Blue Hen's
Chick* many years ago, with the feeling that A. B. Guthrie, Jr.—
after only sixty-three years in this world—had almost given up.
     Indeed, he almost had, but—as one of his colorful Old West
characters might have put it—not quite hardly. At the least, he
was resigned at that point in his personal and literary life to becoming what he jokingly referred to as "a dignified old man."
     And a low point it was. He was living in 1964 with his sister
in Missoula. Only two years before, he had divorced Harriet Larson, his wife of more than three decades; and divorce, right or

wrong, earns always the stigma of failure. He had not produced a novel since *These Thousand Hills* back in 1956. Fourteen years had slipped by since receiving the Pulitzer Prize for distinguished fiction. Several stints in Hollywood had brought little satisfaction; it had been a dozen years since his Academy Award nomination for best screenplay for *Shane*.

Thinking back and comparing past to present—as writing an autobiography necessarily leads a person to do—Bud must have come to wonder about his future. He'd set some mighty high standards for himself in the "early days" of his forties and fifties, and lately things had been slowing down. Lately, he might indeed have been feeling "deserted and thrown in on himself."

At the end of that melancholic April day back in 1964, Bud Guthrie could not have foreseen that just three years hence he would catch a second wind—a second *life*—in the form of a new family. He could not have known that much of his best and most satisfying work was yet to come. And neither could he have known that it would not be until the end of another April day an eventful *twenty-seven years later* that he would finally greet "the last of life."

But despondent or not, Guthrie remained a tenacious fighter, shoving aside the self-doubts expressed in the final pages of his autobiography and bucking himself up to begin *Arfive*—a semi-autobiographical novel he would later remark couldn't have been written without first working through *The Blue Hen's Chick* "to sort things out."

But progress on the new novel was painful and slow, and by 1967 Guthrie was not yet midway through *Arfive* . . . when his fortunes changed: he met Carol Luthin, an intelligent and attractive lady thirty years his junior. In 1969, after a brief but cautious courtship, and only after a great deal of mutual self-examination, Bud and Carol were married—a "risk" neither would ever come to regret.

Crediting Carol as "the best critic I've encountered in a long lifetime," Bud was renewed in energy and self-confidence; now, he returned to his old Corona typing machine with a youthful vigor. His reward: the release of *Arfive* in 1970 to both popular and critical applause, culminating in the prestigious Western Heritage Award.

Gradually, a new life took shape. With Carol's children—Herb and Amy—in high school, the Guthries settled in Missoula, moving to Twin Lakes, near Choteau, for the summers. Bud's concern about being a stepfather was needless; his relationship with the children was easy and loving—a bond that would continue to deepen with the years. His spirits high, he settled back into a productive working schedule.

Across the next two decades, Bud Guthrie would produce a treasure of literary product: 1973—*Once upon a Pond,* a delightful children's book illustrated by Carol and starring a lovable grizzly bear who speaks with the accent of a mountain man; 1973—*Wild Pitch,* the first of a five-novel series of contemporary western mysteries; 1975—*The Last Valley,* an eloquent and prophetic sequel to *Arfive* and the chronological finale to the westering saga that had opened back in 1947 with *The Big Sky;* 1977—*The Genuine Article;* 1980—*No Second Wind;* 1982—*Fair Land, Fair Land,* a requiem for wilderness; 1985—*Playing Catch-Up;* 1987—*Four Miles from Ear Mountain,* an elegant little limited-edition chapbook; 1988—*Big Sky, Fair Land: The Environmental Essays of A. B. Guthrie, Jr.,* which I edited and introduced; 1990—*Murder in the Cotswolds;* 1991—*A Field Guide to Writing Fiction,* an appropriate capstone to a long and distinguished literary career, released—not by design—simultaneously with the author's death.

And fingered in between these dozen "late life" books were scores of newspaper and magazine essays, countless forewords and introductions to the books of respected others, as well as tightly written texts for many courageous and rousing speeches delivered around Montana in the 1970s and '80s on behalf of the environment.

The environment.

Bud was repelled by the biblical exhortation that the earth was made for man, finding such advice simultaneously hubristic and self-destructive. He believed instead that man should view and comport himself as an integral *part of* nature, rather than some divinely ordained taskmaster. Working from that belief, he fought long and hard against the clear-cutting, overgrazing, and strip-mining of public lands, against the damming of free-running rivers for myopic economic goals, against persecution of the grizzly bear and other large predators, against the destructive greed of real-estate developers, and more. Edward Abbey could easily have had the environmental battles of his friend Bud Guthrie in mind when he said, "To disparage the bad is our duty to the good."

But Guthrie was no mere critic; he brought an equal energy to the *support* of those things he viewed as right and good: a sensible moderation of human numbers; the rights of women to control their own bodies and destinies; a cautionary approach to economic growth and "progress"—from which, he was quick to point out, there is no retreat, no going back, right or wrong. Progress is a word, Bud was fond of saying, that should imply an improvement in the *quality* of life, but rarely does.

Although these and others of Guthrie's personal fights most often were neglected by the media in favor of his celebrity as the grand old man of western literature, his altruistic efforts did not go unnoticed: In 1988, A. B. Guthrie, Jr. was named Montana's Environmentalist of the Year—an honor he reckoned as being on a level with his Pulitzer, his several honorary doctorates, and the other major achievements of his life.

And for all of this—the personal honors, the continued success of his books, as well as his broader "unearned happiness"— Bud shared credit with Carol. Everyone who knew them, knew them as inseparable partners; it was always "Bud and Carol."

Alone now, Carol still lives at The Barn, a neat brown frame house along the Teton River where, the first time I ever saw them, she and Bud were standing out front, hand-in-hand, waiting to greet their visitor.

The Barn.

Bud and Carol designed the place themselves and, mindful of its appearance from a distance, dubbed it The Barn. But somehow these days—even with its comfortable familiarity, its warm memories, its full-wall westward view of Ear Mountain looming big as eternity up along the Chinese Wall—somehow, The Barn just isn't the same.

Carol reflects: "Implicit in our marriage was the knowledge that Bud would die first—that I would be left alone. Now that the first shock is over I think I'd be a pretty poor specimen to bemoan my situation. I am grateful for what we had together. What lies ahead I'll meet—sometimes well, sometimes not. What lies ahead is life."

Back when they were married, naysayers had predicted a brief run for such a "mixed" bonding of a not-so "dignified old man" of sixty-eight with what one snippy gossip columnist dismissed as a woman of only thirty-eight. Even his own family found it hard to accept. But Bud and Carol had talked through the potential snags well beforehand. Consequently, "the only problem with our age difference," Carol feels now, "was that had Buddie been younger, he'd still be here with me."

For more than two decades following their marriage, Carol was not just wife and near-constant companion, trusted advisor and literary critic, but a stern shield against a never-ending stream of would-be interlopers who might unnecessarily tax her husband's energies or attempt to use his fame and reputation for their own purposes. And, toward the end, Carol assumed as well the difficult and painful role of bedside nurse. She insists, though, that their marriage was no one-way street. "I needed Buddie," she'll tell you, "every bit as much as he needed me."

To this mutual need Bud was not blind. In a 1980 essay titled "On Marrying A Younger Woman," he expressed strong concern for Carol's happiness and welfare after he was gone:

> A shadow lies in our sunlight. It is the shadow of leaving Carol, as the actuarial tables say I will. Perhaps I was right in that long-ago in warning her against likelihoods. When, once in a while I feel a bit under the weather, I see fright in her eyes. I see dread. I see the hollow years after my death, and I pray that she will meet a man deserving of her, a man who loves goodness.
>
> Lines of old songs, of almost forgotten dance tunes and Methodist hymns I learned as a boy often run in my head. Is it significant that the words, unbidden, that come oftenest to me are . . . "Faretheewell, for I must leave thee. Do not let the parting grieve thee."

Certainly, Bud Guthrie's final quarter-century was extraordinarily blest, filled to the brim with loving family, with continued literary success, with travel—including an extensive working tour of Europe for the U.S. State Department—with public recognition, and with good battles fought and often enough won. Yet, it would be unfair to leave the impression that those years were universally halcyon. No writer's life is without peril or uncertainty. Finances were occasionally a worry. The deaths of his last surviving brother and sister affected Bud deeply. Giving up his beloved Twin Lakes was a wrench, although building The Barn did much to mitigate that. Additionally, with age came increasing physical problems, and Bud became no stranger to pain.

Pain: in 1973, while in the midst of writing *The Last Valley,* problems arising from diminished blood circulation forced Guthrie to undergo arterial bypasses in both legs, an arduous and delicate surgery performed by the renowned heart specialist Dr. Michael DeBakey. Bud's main concern? That it would interfere with his deadline.

Over the years, he survived pneumonia, major surgery for an intestinal blockage, two operations on his shoulder for a basal cell carcinoma, an attack of arteritis, and a frantic trip to the hospital with two bleeding ulcers. Not merely surviving, he always seemed able to regain his old zest and enthusiasm.

In 1986, at the age of eighty-five, after an odds-defying seventy years as a heavy smoker, Bud simply quit; three months later, his doctors prescribed supplemental oxygen. Although he often grumped that the oxygen apparatus made him feel like a "tethered horse," Bud would be dependent on oxygen for the remaining five years of his life. Dependent but not incapacitated. He continued to write and to live an almost normal life. A newspaper article during those years carried the headline, "Bud Guthrie Running on Outrage."

Then, in 1990, the cause of a mysterious pain in the legs was diagnosed as the beginnings of prostate cancer.

Through all of this, Bud Guthrie remained stoic, even cheerful. In a decade of regular correspondence with Bud—a correspondence that generated well in excess of a hundred letters in each direction—he rarely acknowledged, much less complained of, his medical problems, and referred to his hospitalizations, when he mentioned them at all, as mere inconveniences. And—

bless his tough old hide—he never lost his sense of humor. I am reminded of the time, immediately following the diagnosis of prostate cancer, when he wrote, "The experts weren't much worried about the cancer, saying I was so old something else would kill me before it ever could."

That was the Bud Guthrie I knew and loved.

With the decades piling up behind him, and after so many painful close calls, what might have been Bud's thoughts on death? Judging from notes made toward an update of *The Blue Hen's Chick*—an update which, sadly, he would not have time to complete—it seems accurate to describe him as having achieved a bittersweet sense of freedom:

My father always remembered the sense of being free he felt on his first morning in Montana. He meant, I'm sure, free under that great arch of sky, free in the uncluttered distances, free to live free.

As he was in his youth, so I am free in my age, free like him under the big sky and free in directions he didn't mean. The years bring some benefits, not counting the scant consolation that if anything goes wrong with you, it won't be chicken pox. The quick and mortifying embarrassments of the young days are gone, along with the dread of gaucheries and the exalted respect for public opinion. The fierce compulsion of the glands diminishes. So I call these losses gains. At my age I know what I am and where I stand, and if it occurs to me that I could have done better, it is too late to do better now. I settle with myself.

I am free of most encumbrances, so I am free of regret, the most debilitating of indulgences. If you must be regretful, regret what you didn't do, not what you did. A man lets too many smiling opportunities pass him by.

I should add to the other freedoms age has brought me the freedom from the fear of death. At my age it is not far off, and I accept that fact as I must. I do not dread it but neither do I welcome it. What misgivings I have, have not to do with myself but with those I love and who love me. I cannot command them not to mourn, neither in death can I help or advise them. I do not like to think of death for thinking of them. Life demands that we learn to say good-bye.

For myself, again as a writer and a man, I believe in greeting life with a large embrace, full well knowing how fickle it can be, how treacherous, how beset with blind evil, but knowing it can be tender, too, and joyous and loving, and the more rewarding because it can be so unkind. I see heroes along the way, and the sun bright on the hills, and a pretty girl passes me, not unnoticed, and I know what lies ahead and I will meet it with a laugh or a curse, but not, as Cromwell would say, not by the bowels of Christ, with a whimper.

In the fall of 1990, fearing for the first time an isolated Montana winter at The Barn—and The Barn *is* isolated—Bud and Carol went to stay in Bismarck, North Dakota, where Carol's daughter Amy and her family were living. The winter was a hard one even in the city, and Bud was weakening. They returned to The Barn as soon as possible in the spring. Three days after their arrival, Bud collapsed.

During a short hospitalization, sensing what lay ahead, Bud expressed a wish to return to The Barn; Carol brought him home to the mountains.

A few days later, Alfred Bertram Guthrie, Jr., aged ninety years, was gone, his body worn plumb out from nearly a century of living and loving and fighting the good fights.

According to his wishes, his body was cremated and the ashes scattered over Ear Mountain and the adjacent country he had known and loved and written of so evocatively for so very long.

The private memorial service opened with a tribute written by Carol's son, Herb Luthin:

Bud Guthrie hated pomp, no matter what the circumstances, and ostentation did not appeal to him. That's why this service is going to be short—simple. Even calling it a service might shy him away, so let's just think of ourselves as a gathering—a gathering of family and friends, all dear, come to honor him and say farewell: Farewell to Bud Guthrie. Words were his love, his business—his life. So with words we will salute him.

All this country round us was his home. He was a child of the small western town laid out below us—his roots there grew strong and deep. To the west are the mountains that were the backbone of his work. In that range, one peak stands out: Ear Mountain. In its shadow he lived his life and wrote his books. He called Ear Mountain his hold on the universe. It holds him now.

In the early days of Choteau, Bud's father, A. B. Guthrie, Sr., served on the Cemetery Board. This was a bare hillside then, like all the bench slopes on the plains along the Front—burnt in the summer, blasted by wind in the winter. Bud's father, with little loved ones buried here, undertook the planting of these trees, to make some shade and shelter for the graves. When he was a boy, Bud's summer job was to carry water to the young trees. Those trees grew tall and well.

Bud's mother and father are here, as well as brothers and sisters. And so it's here, near the spot where his family rests, that we chose to meet today.

In *The Blue Hen's Chick,* recollecting his father, Bud wrote, "I go to the family graveyard and read the inscription on a stone my father put here after most of us were dead and he had come to live alone." And he goes on to quote the inscription, a poem by Richardson. Bud often repeated these lines—though they haunted him—as he cast back, thinking of his family. As we hear them now, let us think, this time, of him.

> "Warm summer sun,
> Shine kindly here;
> Warm southern wind,
> Blow softly here;
> Green sod above,
> Lie light, lie light.
> Good night, dear hearts,
> Good night, good night."

Yes . . . good night Bud. And thank you. Thank you.

September 1992